MW00636969

FAST TRACK UP
THE CORPORATE LADDER

The 8 Step Guide to
Turbo Charge Your Career

By Len Schutzman
Former PepsiCo Senior Executive

© 2016 by Leonard Schutzman

ALL RIGHTS RESERVED UNDER INTERNATIONAL AND
PAN-AMERICAN COPYRIGHT CONVENTIONS:

No part of this work may be reproduced or transmitted in any form
by any means, electronic or mechanical, including photocopying and
recording, or by any information storage or retrieval system as may be
expressly permitted by the 1976 Copyright Act or as expressly permitted
in writing by the publisher.

Requests for permission should be addressed to:

Leonard Schutzman

6380 Falcon Lair Dr.

Northport FL 34287

Telephone: (941) 423 0283

Email: Len@FastTrackUp.com

www.FastTrackUp.com

The author of this book, Leonard Schutzman, has provided information
and techniques to help you enhance and accelerate your career path. The
author and publisher take no responsibility for the manner in which
this information is utilized, nor do they assume liability for any actions
or for the results of those actions, which you may take as a result of the
information herein contained.

Printed in the U.S.A.

ISBN: 978-1-5136136-2-8
First Edition Printing 2016

CONTENTS

Introduction v

1. From Bean Counter to CFO 1
2. Step #1 Take Control and Seize the Initiative 11
3. Step #2 Broaden Your Horizons 21
4. Step #3 Step Up to the Challenge 33
5. Step #4 Integrity Above All Else 51
6. Step #5 Get Involved in Acquisitions 59
7. Step #6 Build Strong Relationships with Your Network ... 75
8. Step #7 Learn from the Masters by Finding a Mentor 89
9. Step #8 Attract and Develop Future Leaders 103
10. Work and Life Balance 119
11. Life after PepsiCo 125
12. The Eight Step Guide to Turbo Charge Your Career 129

About the Author 139
Acknowledgments 141

Appendix One:
   Len Schutzman's Career Track Record at PepsiCo 143
Appendix Two:
   Individuals Mentored by Len Schutzman Who
   Became Senior Executives in Large Corporations 145

The Career Readiness Education Program 147

WHAT OTHERS ARE SAYING ABOUT
"FAST TRACK UP THE CORPORATE LADDER"

"While there are many books written on leadership, this book is unique in providing practical steps it takes to move into the C-Suite job. Len not only made these moves himself, but helped students and alumni at University of Rochester for many years so the same thing. He has a proven track record."

Andrew Ainslie, Dean, Simon Graduate School of Business

"*The Wall Street Journal* recognized PepsiCo as a place "Where Finance Stars are Born." This book explains why and shares the experiences and insights of my colleague, Len Schutzman, who served in a variety of senior financial positions."

John Bronson, former senior HR executive at PepsiCo,
Frito Lay and Williams Sonoma

"This book contains a wealth of practical ideas on how to become an impactful leader and executive. This is a 'must read' for those who consider themselves stuck in career, as well as those who believe they have potential; far above their current position."

Larry Meyer- President, Uniqlo-U.S.
former CFO Forever 21, Toys R Us International and Gymboree

"As someone who made the journey from bean counter to CFO and CEO, this book is right on point on how to manage your career."

Steve Holmes, Chief Executive Officer, Wyndham Worldwide

"As a representative of the numerous PepsiCo finance alums who worked for Len, this book captures the essence of his eight-step approach to turbocharge you career. His advice and coaching were responsible for positioning me into senior financial positions."

Bob Mayerson- Former Controller and Treasurer of Staples
and Chief Operating Officer and CFO Eastern Mountain Sports

INTRODUCTION

I reached the pinnacle of corporate success at one of the top Fortune 100 companies in the world—and now I want to help you do the same. This book is about my remarkable story, the lessons I learned, and how you can use them to catapult your career.

Fresh out of graduate school, I started out as a low-level bean counter at a large accounting firm. Then I joined PepsiCo and in just three years became the company's Senior VP and Controller, one of the youngest Controllers ever appointed at a multi-billion dollar company at that time.

Before age forty, I served as chief financial officer during restructuring and turnaround challenges in two of PepsiCo's most important businesses, Frito-Lay and Pepsi Cola International. And then, as treasurer, I guided the company's worldwide financing and acquisitions during very active periods in PepsiCo's history.

How did I do it?

Friends regularly marveled at how lucky I was during my career at PepsiCo, but my fast track up the corporate ladder was no accident. Instead, my "luck" was a combination of being fully prepared and knowing how to take advantage of opportunities when they came my way. Luck doesn't come falling out of the sky. You create it.

PepsiCo was a great training ground for me, a demanding culture of exceptionally bright and motivated individuals. It was a "no bullshit" environment that encouraged "outside-the-box" thinking and prudent risk-taking. In 2013, the *Wall Street Journal* cited PepsiCo as a terrific CFO "incubator," a role played by only a select group of companies.

Now I want to share the many lessons I learned in that incubator, so you too can create "luck" for yourself and fast-track your career.

I've developed an eight-step plan for success in the corporate world—a specific program that not only turbo-charged my career, but that I used to mentor dozens of protégés who became top executives at major companies around the world. If it worked for them, it can work for you too!

When I say that PepsiCo was a demanding, "no-bullshit" environment, I'm not exaggerating. I learned that the hard way on a Monday afternoon many years ago. My office was remarkable, with big windows looking out over a lovely sculpture garden, but I didn't have much time to enjoy the view that day. I was up to my ears in paperwork, and when someone knocked, I muttered, "Come in."

When I looked up, it was Andy Pearson, PepsiCo's president. I felt more than a little nervous. Usually, he summoned employees to the executive floor if he wanted to speak with us. This was the first time he'd ever come to see me in my office.

"Hi, Len," he said, pointedly closing the door behind him. "How are you doing today?"

"I'm doing great, Andy. How about you?"

"I'm good, thanks," he responded, then paused. My curiosity, along with my nervousness, jumped another notch. Fortunately, Andy didn't leave me in the dark for long.

"I have a very important assignment for you. I just got off the phone with Bob McKay." McKay was the President of Taco Bell. He and Andy knew each other, as Taco Bell was a major customer of Pepsi.

Andy continued: "Bob has received an offer from a food company to take over Taco Bell. Their Board is inclined to accept the offer, but Bob's reluctant because he doesn't have much confidence in the bidding company—they don't have any restaurant experience. He convinced his Board this morning to give him a very short timeframe to find an alternative buyer." He slipped his hands in his pockets. "Bob thought we might be interested, and I committed to an accelerated review and a preliminary expression of interest in three days."

"Who has been working on this?" I asked, intrigued to find out the numbers.

Before I could say anything more, Andy replied, "My assistant has booked your flight to Los Angeles with American Airlines. It leaves at 4 p.m. It's 2:30 now. You'd better hustle home and pack some clothes."

"Who is coming with me?"

"You're the only person we're sending to California, Len. If we don't make a bid quickly, Taco Bell will accept the other offer." And with that, he turned and left my office.

To say that I felt a little overwhelmed would be a huge understatement. I'd been with the company for only two years and was just thirty-two years old. I was a junior level officer at PepsiCo. As the assistant corporate controller, I handled the accounting and reporting. Now I was being asked to decide whether PepsiCo should make a major acquisition that could have enormous consequences for the company.

How could I gather all the complicated information I needed to formulate an offer in seventy-two hours? Monday was already halfway over, and we'd have to give Taco Bell an answer on Wednesday. It seemed impossible.

"Can't we get more time?" I wondered.

Welcome to my high-stakes world in the amazing corporate culture of PepsiCo!

As you can see, the lessons in this book were not learned in business school but in dozens of high-pressure situations in the executive suites of a billion-dollar company. As one former PepsiCo HR executive put it, "If we throw someone into deep water and he or she is able to survive and flourish, we have exponentially accelerated his or her career development."

That, in a nutshell, is what happened to me, and that is exactly what this book will do for you.

The eight key universal themes that I've distilled from my experience will allow you to accelerate your career in ways you never imagined. You'll learn how to separate yourself from the pack and get noticed! There is so much more you can do to fast-track your corporate career than you might think. *When you're willing to learn and apply the steps I teach you in this book, opportunities you never anticipated will open up for you, just as they did for me.*

Are you ready to fast-track your corporate career? Are you ready for an insider's view of what it takes to succeed? Are you ready to shift into the fast lane?

Turn the page, and let's get started!

The Eight Step Guide to Turbo Charge Your Career

Step #1. Take Control and Seize the Initiative. When I was just thirty-two, PepsiCo gave me three short days to determine whether the company ought to spend hundreds of millions of dollars to purchase Taco Bell. Even though I had never handled an assignment of that magnitude, I realized it was a once-in-a-lifetime opportunity that could change my career. And the same can happen to you. It's not true that an accountant can only be the head of accounting and not the CFO. My career is proof of that.

Step #2. Broaden Your Horizons. Be ahead of the game. Review competitors' websites, read publications, keep abreast of developments in your field, and learn as much about your business and the industry as possible. At the same time, learn how to establish connections with key colleagues. When you broaden your perspective using my techniques, you'll be able to anticipate and benefit from upcoming trends, which will turbo-charge your career.

Step #3. Step Up to the Challenge. Be willing to take on tough, non-traditional jobs or challenging situations that may seem daunting at first. That's what happened to me when I was called upon to address a financial reporting crisis in PepsiCo's international bottling units. By taking on these kinds of challenges, you can significantly enhance your reputation and set yourself apart from the crowd.

Step #4. Have Integrity, No Matter What. Integrity is the bedrock quality for any senior executive. It means objectively providing the facts and "telling it like it is" without sugarcoating, no matter what the consequences might be. When you have integrity above all else, people will have confidence in you. It's the foundation for any successful career.

Step #5. Get Involved in Acquisitions. By contributing to special projects in high visibility areas, such as acquisitions and international business development, you can shine in the eyes of senior management and propel your career to new heights. That's what happened to me when I was involved in the Taco Bell acquisition and during many other acquisitions throughout my career.

Step #6. Build Strong Relationships with Your Network. It was not just the connections I made that contributed to my career; it was developing and nourishing those relationships, year after year, and finding ways to add value to them that made the difference. The people in your network are your conduits to the outside world. They can provide you with the knowledge that gives you power—if you apply the strategies I share.

Step #7. Learn from the Masters by Finding a Mentor. Finding the right mentor was a key factor in my career success, and it can be the same in your career development and entry into higher management. I was fortunate to have had amazing bosses at PepsiCo, each considered a titan in his field. They taught me every aspect of the business. In addition, as a junior executive, you need to understand the etiquette, politics, and unwritten rules of your company's culture if you want to progress up the ranks. A mentor can help you do that.

Step #8. Develop Future Leaders. Developing future leaders not only benefits the company but will help you accelerate your ascent up the corporate ladder. Early in my career, I volunteered to accompany our recruiters on their campus visits to identify talent, and in my networking, I was always on the lookout for people who would be a good fit for PepsiCo. The ability to attract, develop, and retain exceptional talent is an important factor in being considered for senior leadership promotions.

Chapter One

From Bean
Counter to CFO

I t was 3:45 p.m. I was on my plane to L.A. It was now up to me—and me alone—to decide, within the next seventy-two hours, whether or not PepsiCo should acquire Taco Bell. I was just thirty-two years old and never would have thought I'd be given the assignment to determine whether the company ought to spend hundreds of millions of dollars for a major acquisition. I realized it was a once-in-a-lifetime opportunity that could boost my career in ways I never could have imagined—or break it, if I gave the wrong advice. I'm a little Jewish kid from Queens. Mexican food is not what I grew up eating. I knew nothing about Taco Bell. I had never eaten in one.

During the flight, I asked the crew not to bring me any drinks or food. I had to get focused. I thumbed through the financials and quickly realized that with such tight time constraints, my priority must be to identify the key issues and questions. There was no time to waste on anything that wasn't crucial to the deal. Before the plane landed in Los Angeles, I had to develop a solid strategy that would allow me to obtain all the information I needed before the deadline. So for the six-hour flight, all I did was sit and ponder the most important questions I had to ask about the deal. The time went by fast. Before I knew it, the plane was descending.

When I got into the limo at Los Angeles Airport, I asked the driver to take me to the nearest Taco Bell. I needed to find out the basics about Taco Bell, from the ground up. And the best way to do that was in the front lines of their restaurants, not in their corporate suites.

Ordering Everything on the Menu

Just imagine the look on the face of the guy behind the counter when I told him I wanted to order everything on the menu. Now imagine the look on *my* face when I discovered how good the food was! In those days, a taco was only 29¢. It contained meat, cheese, and lettuce, just like a hamburger, but with a crunchy "bun." I was impressed by the satisfying mix of textures and flavors that came at such a low price.

We stopped at every Taco Bell between the airport and my hotel in Irvine, and I sampled food at each one, taking a bite of every item and scribbling notes as we drove to the next outlet. There were about twenty-five to thirty-five Taco Bells between the airport and Irvine, and I ordered the entire menu at every single one. Needless to say, I wasn't very hungry when dinnertime rolled around, but I had gained valuable information.

Besides tasting the food, I saw up front how the restaurants operated, and I made some interesting observations. The food was great, and yet it was made with a limited number of ingredients. The burrito and the taco had the same ingredients, so it was an easy operation and made it very efficient to operate the kitchen. Everything Taco Bell offered was at a very low price point; there were only a few products that cost more than a dollar. It was a quality offering at a good price for the customer. I was impressed.

When we finally made it to the hotel, I was dead tired. It was midnight PST, but my east coast body thought it was 3 a.m. Still, I found it difficult to sleep. I woke up at 4 a.m. PST (7 a.m. EST) and for almost four hours I paced the room, running facts and figures through my head and wishing for the clock to move faster. I finally gave up, got dressed, and went downstairs to wait in the lobby for David Sagal, the controller of Taco Bell.

When he arrived to pick me up, he asked, "Are you hungry? Why don't we stop by a Taco Bell on the way to the office?"

Still stuffed from all the tacos, burritos, tostados, and Bellbeefers I had sampled the night before, I politely passed. "Thanks, but I saw them all yesterday."

David practically did a double-take. "You've seen them all? There are about twenty-five Taco Bells in this area!"

I smiled and patted my stomach. "Sounds about right. I ate at all the ones between here and the airport."

"No wonder you're not hungry. That's a lot of Mexican food."

"Yes," I agreed, "but it was good!"

I was pleased when he laughed.

Outnumbered

At the headquarters of Taco Bell, I was escorted to a conference room. David, being my primary contact person, introduced me to Bob McKay, the president of Taco Bell, their lawyer Jerry Kaplan, and the investment bankers and members of the senior management team who were also in the room.

"Welcome to Taco Bell, Len," Jerry Kaplan said as he shook my hand. "I'm the corporate attorney and one of the members of the senior management team. When is the rest of your team arriving?"

"It's just me, Jerry," I said with a laugh. "I *am* the team."

I was kind of outnumbered. The philosophy of PepsiCo was, "One ranger, one riot." So here I was, all by myself in a room full of people, with everything resting on my shoulders. I could see it was hard for them to believe that PepsiCo would send one lone person to make such an important decision, but Jerry took it in stride.

"Then let's get to it," he said. "Our financial team has gathered the key information for you to review. I recommend you start with these." He handed me a stack of papers. "Let's get you some coffee. Sugar? Milk?" Jerry seemed like the kind of person who took the lead no matter what needed to get done. "We'll stay in the room with you in case you have any questions."

I sat there holding the stack of papers, trying not to stare at the boxes and boxes of additional files piled up all over the floor. There was no way I'd be able to go through all these documents in three days to assess the value of the company and determine whether it would be a good acquisition for PepsiCo. Fortunately, I had no intention of even trying.

Focusing on the Essentials

During the flight to Los Angeles, I had reflected on my approach. The executive team of PepsiCo had put their full trust in me, and I was not going to let them down. They could have selected anyone to go, yet they had chosen me and only me. That fact, plus the time limit, had forced me to pare my entire evaluation process down to its most vital components.

So, to everyone's surprise, I didn't immediately dive into the documents Jerry had just handed me. I took a sip of my coffee, set the stack of papers aside, and turned to David, the controller.

"David, there are only three things I need," I said. "Number one, I'd like to see the financials of the best Taco Bell market in the system. Second, I want to see the ranking of restaurants, high to low volume, sales volume by market. What is your best market, your second best market, etc.? If you could, please give me the top twenty-five markets. Third, I need to know the basic business economics. What is the cost of sales? What are the margins for key menu items and for the restaurants overall? What is the return on investment for new restaurants? And what are the economics of franchising—the fees, expenses, and estimated returns to franchisees?"

David nodded, left the room, and came back a few minutes later. "Here's the P&L of the Taco Bell restaurants in Detroit."

"Detroit?" I asked, dumbfounded. I knew Detroit fairly well. The city didn't have a large Mexican-American population. How could it be Taco Bell's best market in terms of average sales per store and margins?

"Yes, we're very popular in Detroit," David assured me.

"Why?" I asked.

Someone on the other side of the room answered. "Customers, especially the workers in the automotive plants, appreciate that we're giving them a lot of good food for a reasonable price."

I knew for a fact that was true. It was exactly what I had observed the day before when I got my first order. Had I not tested the food, I would have had to take that answer at face value.

"Detroit is our number-one market," David added. When I asked him about Los Angeles, he said, "L.A. is somewhere in the middle. Charleston, West Virginia has the reputation for having a lot of fast food restaurants, and we're performing very well there, too. Lots of people work late shifts in the mines. They're hungry when they go home at 2 or 3 a.m., and they like our food." In fact, I later learned that the Charleston unit was the highest volume restaurant in the system at the time.

My underlying premise was to find out if Taco Bell was a regional chain. Was it popular only in markets with large Mexican-American populations, like Texas, Arizona, and California, or might there be national potential? It was my belief that PepsiCo would not be interested in a regional brand.

Seeing the Hidden Potential

From the revenue ranking, I realized that Taco Bell's attraction wasn't an ethnic thing. It confirmed that the company's market was the blue-collar Quick Service Restaurant consumer. If tacos could make it in Detroit, the restaurant could expand to many other cities with the same profile.

"How many restaurants do you have in Detroit?" I asked.

David scrolled through some papers and answered, "Fifteen. The Detroit population is over 1.5 million." That made me wonder why there weren't more restaurants. David explained, "We open only a limited number of restaurants each year, in order to control our expansion. Our president, Bob McKay, has seen too many concepts that develop more sites than they can properly evaluate and more restaurants than they can effectively supervise each year, only to see many of them fail for lack of business."

Their plan was to open one hundred restaurants per year in new markets. I saw a huge opportunity for even greater expansion. Clustering a larger number of restaurants in existing markets would make advertising and promotion more efficient, and therefore, all the restaurants would benefit. Introducing new restaurants in cities where the Taco Bell brand was less known would require much more effort to reach profit levels.

I knew that if PepsiCo acquired Taco Bell, we would accelerate expansion. If it worked, we would continue. If not, we wouldn't do it again. So I changed the subject to another point that concerned me.

"How come you don't have drive-thrus?" I asked. All successful fast food restaurants had drive-thrus, and it didn't make sense to me why Taco Bell wasn't one of them.

"We've looked into it," President Bob McKay answered, "but Mexican food doesn't travel well. It doesn't taste good when it gets cold." Bob was concerned that the restaurants would lose dine-in customers if customers had a bad take-home experience.

"Well," I said, "couldn't we buy packaging to keep the food warm?" I spoke carefully, afraid that I might offend them with such a simple solution.

"It wouldn't taste the same, though," Bob objected. "If someone had a long drive home, the food still wouldn't stay warm enough to maintain our taste standards."

The fact that Taco Bell didn't have drive-thrus was a huge opportunity, even though the current management didn't agree with me. I wanted them to see that we were on the same page and that PepsiCo could help them, but I didn't want to push too hard, not at this stage.

Bob McKay was a great guy, but it was clear to me that he wasn't comfortable delegating. When I asked him how he decided where to open a new restaurant, his answer was, "I visit each proposed site before we approve it."

I made a mental note. In the world of PepsiCo, it was all about grooming people to take on more responsibility. For Taco Bell to grow, Bob would need to become more comfortable delegating to his key executives.

I continued to ask the questions I had prepared on the plane, and each time I requested new information, someone would leave the room and come back with the exact papers I needed. Even with my preparation and strategy, I couldn't imagine how I would ever wade through all the facts necessary to come to a decision within seventy-two hours, but as the day progressed, I became more and more convinced that I was on the right track.

When Wednesday dawned, the miracle was accomplished—I had all the information I required. I knew that Taco Bell was going to be offered at a fair price. If we didn't offer enough, they would sell to the other buyer. But if I could identify opportunities, we could increase the revenue, and the deal would be worth it.

"Will You Bet Your Career on It?"

Taco Bell's Board meeting was scheduled for the next day, so I had to give my answer soon. A lot had happened since I had arrived, and now it was time to report back to PepsiCo. I used Bob McKay's office to have a conference call with Andy Pearson, the President of PepsiCo, and Don Kendall, the Founder and Chairman of the Board.

"So, Len, tell us what you got," said Andy.

I provided a brief overview of my findings. "The schedule of product margins and economics indicate that there could be a potential for margin improvement by slightly increasing the menu prices, which would still leave us in a favorable competitive position with other fast food chains. However, the franchising analysis indicates that the initial fee structure doesn't provide adequate compensation to Taco Bell for granting the exclusive franchises. They're selling too cheap.

"There are a lot of opportunities for upsides, though. Many Taco Bells don't have dining rooms, only outside seating, and weather doesn't permit people to sit outside throughout the year. They had thought about adding dining rooms, but it costs money. They also don't have drive-thrus. Adding both dining rooms and drive-thrus will significantly increase the revenue."

"Last but not least," I went on, "the attractive return on opening new company-owned stores, particularly by clustering them in high-volume markets, suggests that a shift in development mix to company markets and selective franchise acquisitions could be a source of incremental shareholder value. The numbers clearly indicate that Taco Bell is not a regional chain. Looking at the different opportunities, this can be an incredible transaction for us. We would get a good return on our investment. I can go over the details if you want."

After giving the PepsiCo team the summary of my findings, they were silent for a moment. Then, Andy spoke.

"Len, I have just one question for you."

That was interesting. I had expected that they had done the analysis on their end and would bombard me with questions, making sure I didn't miss anything.

"My question is," Andy continued, "how confident are you of your conclusion? Confident enough to bet your career on it? You see, if we acquire Taco Bell, we'll want you to move to California as its CFO."

I was speechless. This was an exciting opportunity. I didn't mind moving from New York to Los Angeles, but how was I going to convince my eight-months-pregnant wife?

Don, the Founder and Chairman of the Board, chimed in. "Len, what is your answer? Yes or no?"

This was it. If I hesitated, they would think I wasn't sure. I pulled myself together and replied with gusto, "Yes, I'm willing to bet my career on it."

"Great!" Don said with satisfaction. "Get the final deal terms while we poll the Board. You met the seventy-two-hour challenge. Now let's work with Taco Bell to get the agreements in place."

I was thrilled. Who would have thought that the person working as a bean counter at an accounting firm eight years ago would help pull off a major acquisition and be on the path to becoming the CFO of Taco Bell?

TAKEAWAYS!

At the end of each chapter, I'll be summarizing the main points I've made in the form of "takeaways." Here are the key takeaways for the first chapter:

When the Taco Bell opportunity came my way, it once a once-in-a-lifetime chance to accelerate my career. I didn't waste that chance—I was thoroughly prepared and took full advantage of it.

And that is what this book is all about—being fully prepared when the next opportunity comes your way and taking full advantage of it. Positioning yourself for your next promotion is the intersection of preparation and opportunity. And if you know how to prepare yourself, then you won't waste that opportunity.

Through my Eight Steps, I will show you how to make the most of the chances and breaks that come your way. But first, let's review what I did to make the Taco Bell deal work—principles that you can apply to any challenge or opportunity that comes your way, and that will surface again as we go through the Eight Steps:

Takeaway No. 1: Know your business from the ground up. It would have been easy for me to avoid eating at a Taco Bell and just stick to the financials. Whether it's an acquisition situation or your own business, you should know the business from the ground up, from the customer's point of view. The view from the executive suite can be very limited.

Takeaway No. 2: Pare any task down to its essentials. Confronted by my deadline, I had to focus on the most important information needed to accomplish the task. This is what you should do in any high-stakes, high-pressure situation: Focus on the essentials above all else.

Takeaway No. 3: Understand value. By thoroughly acquainting myself with the menu at Taco Bell, as well as its financials, I was able to understand the fundamental value the company offered to its customers. Without that perspective, I would have been operating in the dark.

Takeaway No. 4: Have a long-range strategic view. By looking closely at the company's markets, potential for expansion, and the growth that could be gained by adding drive-thrus and dining rooms, I was able to look beyond the status quo of the present to see the outstanding potential the future offered.

You, too, can turbo-charge your career by being fully prepared when opportunity knocks. All it takes is following the Eight Step process I've developed.

So let's get started with Step One—knowing how to take control and seize the initiative!

Chapter Two

Step #1. Take Control and Seize the Initiative

PepsiCo gave me three short days to determine whether the company ought to spend hundreds of millions of dollars to purchase Taco Bell. Even though I had never handled an assignment of that magnitude, I realized it was a once-in-a-lifetime opportunity that could make my career. And the same can happen to you. It's not true that an accountant can only be the head of accounting and not the CFO. My career is proof of that.

But acquiring Taco Bell was just the start. Now that I was CFO of Taco Bell, I had to help drive the ideas that I had suggested during the acquisition phase. They were no longer just ideas—I had to come up with the strategies and procedures to bring them into reality and increase revenues. I had to put the money where my mouth was. The only way to do that was through Step One: *I had to take control and seize the initiative.*

***

That evening, after I spoke to Don Kendall and Andy Pearson in New York, Bob McKay, David, and I went to a celebratory dinner at Bob's favorite restaurant. The next day the board agreed to accept our offer. Bob called me right away after the board meeting.

"Congratulations Len!" he said, sounding thrilled. "I've heard you're joining us here."

"You better get my office ready, Bob," I responded with a big smile on my face. "I'll be there before you know it."

Even though I was excited, there still was a big hurdle to overcome—I had to tell my wife. I was afraid she would not be happy. All our family and friends lived in the northeast, and asking her to move to the west coast with two little kids and a baby about to be born was a lot to ask. I was pleasantly surprised when she was willing to come along without resistance.

The negotiated contract had the normal two-week due diligence period. David and I worked on the numbers. In the meantime, my wife and I started packing our belongings. The agreement was in place in thirty days, after which a press release had to be sent out and the reports had to be filed with the SEC, as both PepsiCo and Taco Bell were public companies.

In six months, the deal was closed, and my family and I started our new adventure. The move was difficult. We had to sell the house we loved in Connecticut, and it wasn't an easy transition. We discovered quickly that California was very different, and it was difficult to find a house similar to what we were used to. David Sagal, the controller of Taco Bell, and his wife helped us to find a house, and we became good friends.

Putting Ideas into Action

As the CFO of Taco Bell, I was now in the position to be the catalyst for the ideas I had identified to increase revenue. I was in the game, and I loved it. With a little persuasion, Bob McKay was willing to experiment with me and explore the new opportunities. The ideas presented were tested, and we discovered that a lot of the concerns Taco Bell had were unwarranted.

For example, the general thought had been that customers who ate at Taco Bell didn't care about their weight and wouldn't drink Diet Pepsi. To Taco Bell's surprise, that wasn't the case at all. Soda sales went up just by adding Diet Pepsi to the menu.

A bigger idea was to add drive-thrus to the restaurants. Taco Bell's biggest concern had been that the food wouldn't taste good if it wasn't hot. We designed special packaging that would keep the food warm for a reasonable amount of time and quickly discovered that it was possible to contain the heat well enough for people to enjoy the food.

The next big question was whether customers wanted takeout. Would the drive-thrus attract new customers? We tested them on a small scale, and Bob McKay was surprised at the results. Not only did they attract existing customers who didn't have time to sit down in the restaurant, but also new customers who wanted quick takeout food. Once the word spread that drive-thrus increased sales, all the franchise owners wanted them. After they were proven to be profitable, we rolled them out in California, followed by the rest of the country.

Bob and I were having a blast implementing the new ideas. At times, it took negotiation to convince the franchisees that it was worth investing in order to grow. The older units in California didn't have dining rooms. Adding one required a significant investment from the franchisee, as well as closing down the restaurant for several weeks. Many franchisees didn't want to cooperate. They would tell us, "I'm doing well. My sales are great. Why would I invest in building dining rooms? I'll have no income for several weeks."

We knew that if we wanted to be known and to expand on a larger scale, we needed a consistent image—every Taco Bell should have a dining room and drive-thru. Bob didn't want to force the franchisees to our point of view, so we decided that we would prove the benefit to them. We began by building dining rooms in San Francisco, and it was a huge success. Sales increased significantly, and the majority of the franchise owners now wanted dining rooms.

Nevertheless, some of them could still not see our overall vision. David explained to them that they had to aggressively invest to grow or get out. We bought out those who weren't interested in growing, and we either found a more ambitious franchisee or ran the restaurant ourselves.

The process of building dining rooms and adding drive-thrus took about a year, mainly because of the time needed to obtain permits. Sometimes the local taco seller would come to the hearing to prevent us from getting the permit. At times the city was concerned that the drive-thru would cause traffic congestion if delivery wasn't fast enough. After we demonstrated that it took about a minute to get the food ready, that objection was overcome. We were doing a lot of construction. Besides adding dining rooms and drive-thrus, we also built new restaurants and bought other units from franchisees who weren't performing and renovated them. This resulted in a big spike in sales, which was very exciting—these ideas were working, and I was like a kid in a candy store! I had taken control and seized the initiative!

Taco Bell's Real Estate Group began a comprehensive trade area mapping study to determine the unit development potential in each of our biggest markets. They researched in every major city. Where did people live? Where did they shop? How many restaurants already existed? With traffic and population flow, how many stores could we open if we were not concerned about capital costs? What was each restaurant's potential? Based on those findings, we proposed to PepsiCo a major expansion in new restaurant development.

At the time, in the late 1970s, there were less than 500 Taco Bell restaurants in the country. A few years later, there were over 1,200 restaurants. Taco Bell didn't have the capital to expand, but PepsiCo did. A big battleship can't be turned around quickly, but by providing a lot of training, getting franchisees involved in the marketing, and, most importantly, showing them the results, they got behind our expansion plans pretty quick.

Finding Out What the Customer Wants

One day, I was having lunch at the Taco Bell in Irvine. It was close to headquarters, so if Bob and I were not traveling to open new stores or to meet with franchise owners to find out what we could do to support them, you would find me there every single day.

"Good afternoon, Mr. Schutzman, how are you today?" asked Sam, one of the employees.

In the beginning, they weren't sure what to think about my visits, but over time I had made friends with management and employees, to the point that they felt comfortable voicing their complaints and opinions. I'd share my ideas with them and ask them questions about how the business was going.

This time, Jim, the restaurant manager, and some of the other team members joined me while I was having lunch.

"What's new, Len?" Jim asked. "Any exciting new ideas you're going to share with us today? It's amazing how much adding the drive-thru and the dining room has increased our sales volume. I never expected it would make such a big difference. It really was worth the investment."

"Great to hear, Jim!" I said. "It's been a success all over the country. Now, the question is: What's next? How can we serve our customers even better, so we get them to keep coming back? Do you have any suggestions?"

As I asked this question, I was looking around at the rest of Jim's team. They were in the restaurant day in and day out. They knew what their customers liked best.

"All I know is that people love the Burrito and the Taco," said Jillian. She was a long-time employee, and the customers adored her. "What if we could offer them a Super Burrito? We'll be able to charge more." She smiled at me, knowing that I'd like her business-oriented thinking.

"That is a brilliant idea, Jillian! Any thoughts, Jim?"

"She's right," Jim agreed. "The Burrito and the Taco are our all-time bestsellers."

"Let's see what we can do," I said. "I really like the idea."

That day, the Burrito Supreme and the Taco Supreme were born. That was one of our smaller wins but nevertheless contributed to increased sales. We added extra ingredients and sour cream, and they became a big hit! I loved them so much that I ate them for lunch for the next year—even on weekends.

Burned by Overconfidence

A big part of Step One is not losing the initiative by taking unneeded risks. It's great when your ideas are successful and you're flying high, but you also run the risk of getting overconfident and making mistakes. I learned that the hard way.

"Two chilies, please." I was placing the order in our new Taco Bell restaurant on Long Island. Andy Pearson had come to visit, and I was excited to share my latest idea with him.

"Chili will be a great new addition to the menu, Andy," I said. "People will love it!"

I handed him his chili while we walked to a table. We had recently opened four new stores in New York, but they weren't doing as well as we had expected. The problem was that New Yorkers were not familiar with tacos and burritos, so we came up with an idea to solve the problem. I knew that another chain sold chili, but theirs was made from leftover hamburger meat. We developed a great chili recipe made with fresh meat.

"Where's the market research, Len?" Andy asked. "Did you test it?"

"You didn't taste it yet?" I responded, as proud as the father of a newborn child. "It's amazing! Of course the customers will love it. I'm confident it will be a success."

Andy burst my bubble. "Even though it tastes good, we always have to find out what our customers want."

Unfortunately, Andy turned out to be right. We were not "Chili Bell." We were Taco Bell, and I quickly discovered that although some of our existing customers would order it, "our delicious chili" didn't bring us new sales.

Every new idea we had introduced up to now had proven to be successful, and I assumed this idea would work, too. I learned a valuable lesson: You can't make decisions based on what you like. You have to test and find out what your customers want.

Bob and I would go into restaurants to help the crew, and from what we learned, we made little tweaks to improve the operating system, which allowed them to deliver a great product with even greater speed.

Seeking Solutions at the Ground Level

People in your organization will have great ideas, but they have to be empowered to put those ideas into action. They have to know that their ideas matter.

When Bob and I visited restaurants, we'd get the teams together to find out what was happening on the front lines. We'd say to them, "You guys are doing this every day. That's your job. You tell us—how can we do this better? What can we do to make your life easier? We want to give you the tools to do a better job."

We wanted the input of our teams. We wanted to let them loose and encourage their creativity. In each restaurant, we gave them a challenge and offered them small incentives to come up with new ideas. There's a lot of value in asking the workers how they can do their jobs better and more quickly, without affecting the overall quality.

At Taco Bell, nobody had previously looked at engineering the line, because, in most of the food industry, it's a simple process. If you're making a hamburger or you're making fried chicken, it's pretty simple. But with Mexican food, it was more complicated because of our emphasis on fresh, made-to-order meals. We didn't want speed of service to affect the quality of the food. For Taco Bell, speed of service wasn't our main selling point. We didn't want to prepare a taco and put it under a heat lamp.

But with drive-thrus or sit-down fast food restaurants, speed of service is paramount. From doing some research on other chains, which basically involved me talking to my counterparts, we found that people aren't prepared to wait for more than one minute when they order food at a drive-thru.

Speeding up the process without sacrificing quality involved two things. One was trying to use information to better anticipate order flow and peaks in the business. The second was taking a really hard look at what kinds of products Taco Bell offered. Even in those days, we had a pretty good point-of-sale information system that captured what was being ordered by time frame. They call it data mining, which is a hot subject now, where you look at patterns and trends and try to predict what you're going to get. Because once you can predict the order flow, you have a chance of speeding things up.

The data gave us a lot of useful ammunition. People tend to order certain things together. The hamburger analogy would be a burger, fries, and a drink. In our case, it was a burrito, nachos, and a drink.

Knowing what a typical lunch order was, we examined every step that was involved in making the products. How long does each step take? Could two people do it? Or just one person? What was the best way to deliver a product one minute after it was ordered?

STEP #1 TAKEAWAYS!

PepsiCo is a place where they give you lots of opportunity to grow, but if you say you're going to do something, you have to deliver—and we did! I was having the time of my life. What a chance to have such an impact! PepsiCo's Executives came out to see "the new toy." Because I had learned everything about Taco Bell from the ground up, I was no longer perceived as "just the numbers guy." In a short time, I became the Superstar!

That's because I practiced Step One—I took control and seized the initiative. If I came in as "just the numbers guy," I wouldn't have been able to make such an impact on Taco Bell, and I wouldn't have been ready for the next great opportunity beyond being the CFO at Taco Bell.

Here is what I did, and what you can also do, to put Step One into action by taking control and seizing the initiative.

Takeaway No. 1: Be willing to challenge assumptions. Taco Bell assumed they couldn't sell diet soda or profit from drive-thrus or dining areas. By being willing to challenge these assumptions, I helped drive the company's growth. Always be willing to challenge the status quo and look beyond it to spot new and better opportunities.

Takeaway No. 2: Prove the benefits first when making large company changes. We wanted all Taco Bell units to have dining rooms, but we began by building dining rooms in the San Francisco market. It was a huge success. Sales increased significantly, and the majority of the franchise owners then wanted dining rooms. Prove the value of a change on a small scale before making a big change in the way you do business.

Takeaway No. 3: Do your research. Never assume, always test, always find out what the customer wants. While "outside-the-box" thinking and intuition are important, there is no substitute for good market research and testing. When we introduced chili at Taco Bell, we learned a valuable lesson: We couldn't make decisions based on what we liked. It should have been tested first to find out what the customers liked.

Takeaway No. 4: Break down walls between the corporate suite and employees. By establishing trust with your employees, they will become comfortable in voicing their complaints and opinions, which will provide you with valuable information to improve the business.

Takeaway No. 5: Get to know what the customers want on the ground floor. By talking with employees about customer preferences, the Burrito Supreme and Taco Supreme were born, contributing to increased sales. Testing is important, but it's also important to talk to the employees who are doing the job every day and who know what customers want.

Takeaway No. 6: Know what your employees do each day. By knowing firsthand what their jobs are like, you can make little tweaks to improve your operating system, which enables you to deliver great products with even greater efficiency. That is how we increased the speed of service at Taco Bell without sacrificing our great quality.

The Next Step!

Now that I had a solid footing at Taco Bell, I wasn't resting on my laurels. I knew I had to continue to focus on new ways to expand my career. I was always looking ahead, always preparing for the next big opportunity that would one day come my way. And to win that opportunity, I had to put Step Two into action—I had to broaden my horizons.

CHAPTER THREE

STEP #2. BROADEN YOUR HORIZONS

I was happy being CFO of Taco Bell. But I was also aware that I didn't want my career to end there. I knew that one day a bigger and better opportunity would come along. To prepare for that opportunity, I had to employ Step Two. I had to broaden my horizons. I had to learn much more than what was required by my current position at Taco Bell. I had to expand my awareness of developments in my industry and establish connections with key colleagues.

When you broaden your perspective using my techniques, you'll be able to anticipate and benefit from upcoming trends, which will turbo-charge your career.

Let's take a look at how I put Step Two into action.

Tom Galligan had been the first person I recruited for PepsiCo after I joined the company in 1976. He was someone I knew from the accounting firm I had joined after graduate school, so when we had to upgrade the consolidation and financial reporting system at PepsiCo, he was the first person who came to mind. Most people in the group had been doing the same thing for more than twenty years. I needed somebody to drive that effort and be a change agent with leadership skills.

With a Harvard MBA, Tom may have seemed overqualified for the position, yet I knew that he had dreams and aspirations. When I explained to him the opportunity and gave him my personal commitment that I would support his career, he came on board—and he did a great job!

He was working as the director of corporate accounting and financial reporting at PepsiCo, and during our weekly lunch meetings, I would update him on what was going on in the company. By following the blueprint my boss had shared with me and that I had fine-tuned and improved, I showed Tom how to position himself to be a CFO one day and taught him about each business unit. I made sure he'd be invited to the various divisional meetings and senior corporate staff meetings, so the senior management of PepsiCo would get to know him. In short, I was helping Tom to broaden his horizons.

When I was based in New York, Tom and I used to meet for lunch every week. Since I had moved to California, we hadn't talked, so one afternoon I decided to pick up the phone and find out how his career development was going.

"Hello, Len," he greeted me warmly. "How are you? How's it going at Taco Bell?"

"I'm fantastic, Tom. So great to talk to you."

After chatting for a few minutes, Tom said, "Len, you've been such a great mentor. If it weren't for you, I'd still be an accountant at the firm. I know that we have a similar background. What has made you climb the corporate ladders so fast with PepsiCo?"

The Secrets to My Success

I smiled when I heard his question. It was one of those questions that make you proud to be a mentor because it shows that you have an eager protégé who is open to learning. I said to Tom, "There are eight specific steps that will determine your role in the company ten years from now. I will share a very important one with you. You need to broaden your horizons."

I continued, "The only way you stay ahead of the game is when you are up-to-date, when you know what is happening in the industry, and when you watch the trends. You have to get out of your shell. Pay attention to where the market is going and where the company is strategically focused."

I told Tom about the different sources I used to stay informed. As an alumnus of Arthur Young, I established a close relationship with one of their senior partners. He arranged for me to receive their accounting and tax developments newsletter and press releases from foreign offices in major countries where PepsiCo did business (PepsiCo was one of Arthur Young's major clients). That was a great resource that helped me keep an eye on what was happening around the globe.

I also told Tom that, on a weekly basis, I reviewed the websites of important public companies that were our competitors, as well as their press releases and earnings webcasts. I summarized and shared developments with the head of financial planning and counterparts in other staff functions. To keep abreast of current business developments, I read *The Wall Street Journal, Financial Times,* and *The Economist* on a regular basis.

"Yes, I like reading *The Economist,*" Tom said. "It provides great information."

"That is the general information, which is important," I agreed, taking a sip of coffee. "But you want to make sure that you also know exactly what is happening with PepsiCo. That way, you'll be able to add value to your company. For example, I built a relationship with the head of investor relations. He was willing to send me analyst reports issued on PepsiCo and our competitors. That was valuable information to have access too."

"That's a very good idea," Tom responded. "I can see the value of having that important data."

He was a bright guy. What I liked about him most was that he was the kind of person who acts and makes things happen.

It's Not Serendipity but Strategy

Tom was silent for a moment and then said, "Some older colleagues were saying that you were lucky to be selected to be a key senior executive at Taco Bell. One guy even said that it was just because Andy Pearson likes you. He also said you're always trying to be noticed by senior management now that you're CFO of Taco Bell. I think he was just jealous. He's had the same job for ten years, and it doesn't seem that he's going anywhere new in the next ten."

"That's a very good observation," I said. "People will criticize you when you're successful and they're not. What I've shared with you are the guidelines to separate yourself from the crowd. It's the only way you'll progress. You have to show that you have a little more to bring to the table than the next guy."

Tom said, "I'd love to hear the Taco Bell story, though. Why did they choose you? I know it wasn't serendipity."

"You're right. Even though it may look like serendipity on the outside, there was a careful strategy behind it. When I say that it's important to broaden your horizons if you want to climb the corporate ladder, I didn't get that from a book. Everything I'm teaching you is what has worked for me."

I was proud of my protégée's willingness to learn. His "go-getter" mentality is what's needed to succeed in life, regardless of what your career path is. I was happy to share with him what I did behind the scenes to prepare me for this opportunity.

"The key is to think strategically," I told Tom. "You can't get too caught up in the day-to-day tasks. You have to look ahead if you want to be ahead of the game. After the acquisition of Pizza Hut by PepsiCo, I was convinced that PepsiCo would likely try to expand its presence in the restaurant industry. I realized that nobody on the corporate staff had restaurant expertise, and I could become the go-to guy if I did my homework. So I began a program to educate myself about the industry and the key companies. When the Taco Bell opportunity came along, I was ready to jump on it because of all that preparation and planning."

Virtually every industry has a trade publication, and you should make it a point to read them regularly. I subscribed to and read *Nation's Restaurant News*, the primary industry trade publication. Thanks to the connections I had made at Goldman Sachs, where my brother-in-law was a partner, I met their restaurant industry analyst, and he was willing to send me their financial reports. I also reviewed all the reports and information submitted by Pizza Hut. I got myself invited to meetings with analysts. These were people with insights, and I had to get myself into their world.

There's a lot of information that can help you. You just need to find it and commit to mastering it. Every public company holds quarterly conference calls with security analysts. Listening to your company's calls is a "must do." But you shouldn't limit yourself to the conference calls of your own company. You'll gain a lot of insight if you listen to the quarterly conference calls of a range of companies. I wanted to become the expert in fast food restaurants, so I listened to the conference calls of McDonalds, Burger King, and other fast-food chains. They would reveal their margins, and I created a chart that had Taco Bell and Pizza Hut on it. This gave me a much broader perspective on the industry.

Providing Value to Colleagues

After each conference call, I would send out emails about what I had found out to people within PepsiCo who could use that information. One time, I listened to Domino's quarterly conference, where they shared that their online ordering system was up 10 percent. It gave me an excuse to write to strategic planning and share that data with them. You get recognized if you provide value to people within your company. I helped them look better because they forwarded the information to the corporate staff. It was a win-win—I helped the company, but I also clearly helped my reputation as well.

I also checked the websites of all of our public competitors to read their financial reports, listened to their webcasts on earnings, and followed their presentations to analyst groups. I summarized this information, provided comments on possible implications for PepsiCo, and sent what I learned to our strategy and business planning folks. This broader interest caught the eye of other staff professionals and allowed me to expand my network of contacts.

A company's presentation at investment conferences will keep you up-to-date on its performance. Plus, you'll hear about the key issues on the minds of investors. Periodically, companies hold an investor day, where management gives analysts, current investors, and prospective investors a deeper look into their results, strategy, culture, and anything else they feel is important to talk about. You should attend in person if possible or at least listen to the webcast. As my knowledge base increased, I began having regular lunches with my boss and the head of strategic planning to keep abreast of PepsiCo's thinking and to demonstrate my readiness to participate in any potential transactions.

When there was a rumor that KFC would be sold by Heublein, I went into my network to find out if it was true. They told me that Heublein was likely to sell eventually. So, to stay ahead of the game, I'd listen to Heublein's conference calls. When I learned that they had hired an investment bank to sell KFC, we had a head start and could move quickly because I already had done my homework by keeping track of KFC for a while. As a result, PepsiCo bought KFC.

When I told Tom about all the homework I did on a regular basis, he was more excited than ever.

Looking for Ways to Support Management

"What brilliant ideas, Len! This really helps me to understand what's required to position myself as a CFO and how important it is to stay up-to-date about what's happening in the industry."

"You see, Tom, you want to identify emerging trends and innovations. An excellent source to do this is by attending trade shows. It may take me an hour every quarter, and yet it gives me valuable information. I summarized my observations and sent them to the head of strategy at Frito-Lay and to the division business planner at corporate. This was not part of my job description. I'm just always looking for business opportunities."

At this point, I gave Tom a hint about how he could take advantage of an emerging business opportunity. "Right now, PepsiCo is interested in acquiring more bottlers. Because these are very asset-intensive acquisitions, the financial side is going to be more important. If you can dig deep and make it a point to study the bottling business and get to know its economics inside out, it could be a chance for you to display your financial acumen and get noticed by upper management. Stay on top of what other bottlers are doing, including Coke, and study their websites. You have to do your homework and be ready."

"That's a great idea, Len. I hadn't thought of that," said Tom.

"What you have to keep in mind," I continued, "is that PepsiCo's culture is to develop the next generation of leaders. You have to show that you're a leader.

Look for ways you can support management. For example, in addition to the competitive analyses I told you about, I also enhanced financial reports to make them more useful to management. As a supplement to the normal stability reporting, I worked with the business planning group to design trend reports on key performance indicators and reports on cash flow and working capital management. Previously, there were no reports on cash flow and working capital management, and management realized that this data could help them make better decisions. Taking these steps helped me fast-track my career."

I could hear that Tom was fervently taking notes. When I paused, he stopped typing and said, "Wow! I can see that you were very well prepared and that your promotion didn't happen by accident. You studied the industry thoroughly and added value to strategic planning, senior management, and your other contacts by providing them with key information. What surprises me is that the majority of the people aren't willing to do the work, but then they complain that others are being promoted while they're stuck in the same position for years. Thank you for telling me your story. I know you well enough to know that it wasn't luck that got you there, but understanding exactly how you broadened your horizons taught me a lot."

I told Tom that Karl Vonder Heyden, my boss, was a great mentor for me. "Karl recruited me to join PepsiCo as Assistant Corporate Controller. Karl had a passion for developing new talent, but he selected only those individuals who had drive and ambition. Now I, in turn, enjoy mentoring others. So, let me ask you, Tom, are you ready to take the next step in your career?"

"Absolutely!" he responded.

"Okay," I replied. "I'm going to check back with you in two weeks, and I want you to report back to me on the specific steps you've taken to broaden your horizons."

"Thank you, Len. I appreciate it greatly. I remember when you interviewed me for my first job with PepsiCo. You told me that you'd help me grow my career, and you have certainly kept your word."

"I have to go," I said. "I'll be in touch soon to see how things are going."

Tom followed my advice, and he eventually became CFO of Pepsi Cola Bottling Group.

STEP #2. TAKEAWAYS!

To get ahead in your career, get ahead of the game. Learn as much about your business and the industry as possible. Review competitors' websites, read publications, keep abreast of developments in your field. At the same time, learn how to establish connections with key colleagues by providing them with information of value. Don't stand pat. Don't become comfortable with what's in front of you. When you expand your horizons, you expand your career opportunities.

Here are specific steps you can take to implement Step Two.

Takeaway No. 1: Broaden your horizons by being up-to-date about what's happening in your industry and the current trends. To break out of a functional silo and demonstrate your breadth for more senior-level positions, it's essential that you regularly follow the activities of your competitors, listen to webcasts of competitors, and keep abreast of current developments. There's a lot of information that can help you; you just need to find it and make it part of your daily routine.

Takeaway No. 2: Add value to your company and provide value to key colleagues. You get recognized when you provide value to the company as a whole and to specific colleagues. I advanced my career by providing key data and information to strategic planning, senior management, and other contacts, thereby adding value to their work and my own as well.

Takeaway No. 3: Look for ways to get ahead of the competition. I realized that nobody in PepsiCo had restaurant expertise and that I could therefore become the go-to guy if I did my homework. When the Taco Bell opportunity came along, all that homework paid off, and I was prepared to pounce.

Takeaway No. 4: Show that you're a leader by looking for ways to support management. I began having regular lunches with my boss and the head of strategic planning to keep abreast of PepsiCo's thinking and to demonstrate my readiness to participate in any potential transactions that came along. When new opportunities came along, I was on their radar and prepared to take on new responsibilities.

Takeaway No. 5: Be willing to go beyond your job description. Sticking to your job description won't get you new and exciting opportunities. By keeping yourself current on all new developments in your functional area, you'll demonstrate to other executives your broader business knowledge and your willingness to go far beyond your current responsibilities.

Takeaway No. 6: Identify emerging trends and innovations. Keeping abreast of emerging trends can provide meaningful insights into business planning and decision-making. The following is a summary of expected demographic trends that will create opportunities for businesses in the next several decades.

- The explosive growth in the so-called "Millennial Generation," totaling 79 million people between the ages of sixteen and thirty-four, offers new opportunities. These individuals have significantly different interests and attitudes compared to their parents, the Baby Boomer generation. They want to live in luxury buildings in the city, not in the suburbs. A good description of these different interests and beliefs can be found online in the BCG Report on "The Millennial Consumers." Developing products and services for this large and growing market will represent a big opportunity for businesses.

- There will be 90 million Americans over age sixty-five by 2050. The aging of the U.S. population presents opportunities for products and services targeted at this group.

- Ethnic niche markets will continue to grow, particularly for Hispanics and Asians. The Hispanic and Asian populations are growing rapidly, so products targeted to these groups should represent attractive opportunities.

- There is a growing interest in health and wellness, which manifests itself in the explosion of organic and natural foods. It used to be hard to get products like these into distribution. Now, with e-commerce, new and innovative products can be launched and sold both in the U.S. and overseas through the use of online sales and marketing techniques on global platforms like Amazon.com and Alibaba.com.

The Next Step!

My career was going well, and I was excited that Tom Galligan's career was progressing too. But because I had positioned myself for life in the fast lane, my business career was going to change in even greater ways than I ever could have imagined. Little did I know the kinds of difficult challenges I was going to face. And yet I learned, in the next phase of my career, that it was only through the most difficult kinds of challenges that I could fully reach my true potential.

Chapter Four

Step #3. Step Up to the Challenge

It is only by stepping up to the challenge—by being willing to take on tough, non-traditional jobs or challenging situations that may seem daunting at first—that you can fully turbo-charge your career. That's what happened to me when I was called upon to address a financial reporting crisis in PepsiCo's international bottling units. By taking on these kinds of challenges, by putting yourself willingly into the pressure cooker, you can significantly enhance your reputation and set yourself apart from the crowd.

Here's the story of how I put Step Three into action. . . .

The new and old Taco Bell teams blended nicely. We had brought in expertise where we needed it, but we wanted to retain the Taco Bell people as much as possible. We had been careful not to create the impression that we only wanted Pepsi people working for us. We didn't want to upset the people who had worked there for a long time. A few new hires and transfers from other PepsiCo operations had been made to fill in experience gaps in areas such as marketing, training, business planning, legal strategic planning, and human resources management. The Taco Bell people appreciated this, realizing that growth was a huge advantage for the business as well as for them personally.

A Return to New York

While I was having the time of my life immersing myself in the business and being the catalyst for change, my wife was not so happy. She was having a hard time with our new life. She missed her family and friends and didn't want to raise our three young children in southern California. I couldn't convince her to stay.

PepsiCo had spent a lot of money to move us cross-country, and the agreement was that I would be Taco Bell's CFO for three years. Now, within a year, I had to tell them our plans had changed. With a heavy heart, I picked up the phone to call Andy Pearson, the President of PepsiCo, afraid that if I told him I wanted to return to New York it would be a career breaker.

"Hi Andy, how are you? This is Len." I was making an effort to sound as relaxed as possible.

"I'm doing great. How about yourself?"

"Great, thanks," I responded, but Andy knew me well enough to know that wasn't the truth.

"Just tell me the truth, Len," Andy said, a note of concern in his voice. "What's going on? Are there problems at Taco Bell?"

I laughed half-heartedly. "I wish it were a business issue. That would be easier to solve. My wife and I have had many conversations in the last few weeks. She can't adapt to the Californian lifestyle, and she wants us to move back to the east coast. You've given me an amazing opportunity to come out here and be part of the leadership team at Taco Bell, but I have to take care of my family."

Andy responded in a friendly, understanding tone. "Len, you did a terrific job at Taco Bell. I'm grateful for what you have accomplished. Bob McCay has the highest respect for you, and now I know why he thinks so highly of you. You've proven that you understood the business and you got Taco Bell back on the right track."

Even though he was a little disappointed, Andy understood that I was upset and that it wasn't easy for me to leave the position. He continued, "Don't worry about being pigeonholed when you return. After this experience, you'll never be just a bean counter again. I understand that these things happen. I appreciate what you've done, and I'm going to involve you even more with the business when you're back."

"Thank you, Andy. That sounds great!"

I was very relieved that he understood my dilemma. I had been concerned that he would think I was a quitter, but instead he was very accommodating and appreciative.

After I talked with Andy, I called Bob Dettmer, the financial vice president, who was my direct boss, and he was very supportive and understanding as well.

"Your career path has been enhanced," he told me. "Don't see it as a defeat. There will be another great opportunity for you."

Serendipity happened. Two weeks later, Andy called to tell me that the job of corporate controller at PepsiCo would become available. To the outside world, it seemed that I was promoted when they offered me that job because it was a bigger job than CFO at Taco Bell. But to me, having to leave the job I loved and going back to corporate felt like a step backward.

While being in the corporate office seemed to carry a lot of status for some people, I liked being in a business unit where I could make things happen and influence how the business was run. If you're in corporate, you don't get involved in the operating units. As the controller, I didn't have as much influence.

So, I had some reservations about going back to New York, but Andy Pearson, one of my key mentors, was supportive and really clear with me that my life was never going to be the same—in a very good way.

Andy and I met for lunch the first day I was back at the office in New York. He said that I had demonstrated great skill at Taco Bell, and he wanted me to stay involved with them, as well as get involved in other operating units of the company.

He said, "Len, you did a terrific job in Taco Bell. You became the key advisor of Bob McKay. There's a lot going on because of you. They're acquiring franchisees, organizing the taxes, and building their strategic team. Just because you're on the east coast doesn't mean you can't be of value to Taco Bell. You're close to Bob. Stay close to Taco Bell and be the focal point. Coordinate the rest of your team and get them involved as needed."

Andy added, "Don't just think about the numbers—think about business processes, think about acquisitions."

I had a reputation by now because of the acquisitions we had made. I knew how to evaluate companies and how to integrate them into the family. I became Andy's guy. When people said, "We'd like to look at buying another company," Andy would say, "Get Len involved. He's had a lot of experience with this." I'd go out there and work with our teams and give them whatever insights I had.

I reached out to the strategic and business planning groups of Frito-Lay, Pepsi Bottling Group, and Food and Beverage International. I made it a point to stay close to them and attend their monthly strategic planning meetings, so I could stay current with the issues they were facing, find ways to add value to their work, and become involved in their projects. As a result, I continued to open new doors of opportunity.

Cleaning up the Scandal in International Bottling
(1983-1984)

I wasn't back in New York for very long when the next great opportunity came my way. At first, it looked more like a disaster than an opportunity, but this is when I learned the true value of Step Three—stepping up to the challenge.

John Flaherty, PepsiCo's General Auditor, sat down across my desk. He had provided me with the newly issued internal audit reports of several international bottling units. It was my responsibility as the controller to be up to date.

"You were in Mexico not so long ago," I said to John. "What was your observation? I recognize some weaknesses in internal controls in these reports."

"The operations in lesser developed countries often don't have the ethics, business practices, and accounting standards as we do in the U.S.," John answered. "They don't have such a high standard."

John and I discussed the reports a little further, and we decided to go to Mexico together to assess firsthand the management, financial controls, and financial statements. We had our flights booked, and a week later we arrived in Mexico City.

A driver picked us up from the airport and took us to the Camino Real, one of the premier hotels in the Mexico City. As soon as I walked into my hotel room, the phone rang. I picked it up.

"Hello?"

"Good afternoon, sir," replied a heavy voice in a strong Spanish accent. "I am the accounting manager of the Mexican bottling subsidiary. I have concerns about the financial reporting, and I need to speak with you about this as soon as possible."

"Thank you for calling me," I said. "I appreciate it very much. We would like to hear what you have to share with us. Consistent with PepsiCo's whistle-blower policy, you should speak with the general auditor of PepsiCo, John Flaherty. He's in room number 638. Would you be willing to share with him what you just told me?"

The caller agreed.

I finished unpacking and was reviewing the numbers two hours later when the phone rang again. It was John, who had finished meeting with the whistleblower.

"We Have a Big Problem"

"Len, we have a big problem," said John. "There's reason to suspect that the whistleblower has a copy of a schedule with bogus accounting entries to show a higher income. The misstatements were material."

"What?" I responded, astonished.

"Yes, I'm shocked too," John replied. "He gave me a copy of the schedule. He also believes other operations in the international bottling division maintain similar schedules. It seems that they've been cooking the books."

John handed me the schedule. After looking at it, I said, "I suspected that something wasn't right, but I didn't expect the numbers to be so big. If the schedule he gave you is true, PepsiCo could be in big trouble."

"There is no reason not to believe this guy," John said. "The information he provided was very detailed."

"Let's get back to New York on the first flight we can catch. We have to file a report and brief PepsiCo's CFO and the rest of the executive team. Better we meet with them in person than talk over the phone."

A million things were going through my head. Instead of staying for a week as we had initially planned, we packed our suitcases and went straight back to the airport.

Back in New York, I called an emergency meeting the next morning at 8:30 a.m. and told my secretary that she had to make sure everyone I needed would be there, regardless of what other appointments they might have to cancel. Pepsi's General Counsel led the meeting. The representatives of Pepsi's international business division and the lawyers were anxious to find out what was going on.

When John and I explained what had happened in Mexico, they were as shocked as we were. We were well aware of the repercussions this would have for PepsiCo. Once the commotion had settled, the General Counsel said calmly, "Before we take any action, we need to verify that the copy of the schedule is correct. Let's get John and his team to Mexico for an audit." The rest of the executive team agreed.

John returned to Mexico to review the documentation and validate its reliability. In the meantime, I mapped out an action plan to put in effect after John confirmed the fraud we suspected. There were a couple of important steps that had to be taken. The SEC had to be informed, and a press release sent out to inform the public. The next steps would be to replace anyone involved in the cover-up and figure out how to rebuild the international bottling unit. That was not a small task.

John's audit confirmed that the financial statements were wrong and that the whistleblower's schedule indeed indicated fraud. What's more, he received a tip about other countries where the books had been falsified. John sent additional auditing teams to Brazil, Spain, Puerto Rico, Belgium, Japan, and the Philippines. We were in a full-blown crisis.

John and I met with the International Division and the corporate management team to discuss how we were going to clean up the mess. We decided to fly the financial directors from all international units to New York. We felt that if they were away from their operating teams, they were more likely to tell us the truth, which would help us to determine the extent of the problem. When they arrived, we locked everybody in the conference room with the lawyers present.

The financial directors were anxious to find out why we had invested the effort and the expense to fly them in from all over the world. The General Counsel took a direct approach and said, "We have reason to believe that the financial statements have been falsified and there has been some cooking of the books. There is some serious shit going on. If you have a schedule, tell us now. We can't tolerate this. As the financial director, you either know about it or you should have known about it."

I stayed calm, yet the tone of the General Counsel's voice made it clear that this was serious business. The room went deadly quiet. You could have heard a pin drop. Nobody said anything. They looked at one another as if someone else was going to say something. Obviously, they knew they were in trouble—big trouble.

After sitting in silence for several minutes, nobody was willing to confess.

"We'll have to replace everyone in this room," I said. "You'll be put on leave, so we can get to the bottom of this and fix it."

After the meeting was dismissed, the General Counsel and I convened.

"What are your thoughts, Len?" he asked, still shocked at what had taken place.

"We must find out if the fraud originated higher up in their units," I replied. "Since we need their cooperation to figure out who really is responsible, we should transfer the financial directors to administrative roles during the investigation." Bob agreed with this approach.

Once we knew there was reason to believe that the statements were fraudulent, we informed the SEC that investors couldn't rely on those statements. PepsiCo could be sued.

To handle the situation, PepsiCo assigned two individuals with the responsibility to clean up the fiasco. Bob Carlton, a senior financial executive at one of the transportation division units, was appointed corporate controller; he was charged to prepare restated financial statements and handle the expected investigation by the SEC.

Assembling a Crisis Team

I was asked to become the Chief Financial Officer of the newly named Pepsi Cola Bottling International Group. It was my responsibility to build a strong financial team at the division headquarters and at operating units and develop and execute an appropriate business strategy to turn the situation around.

There were investigations, lawsuits, and a lot of pressure. The only international managers retained were the manager in Mexico, who first alerted us about the situation, and a newly appointed finance director in the Philippines; neither had any involvement in the accounting irregularities. We had no other option than to terminate those who knew or should have known what was going on. Because everyone who had any financial knowledge related to international operations had been fired, I had to build a new team from scratch. I felt like the main character in the television series *Mission: Impossible*.

Andy Pearson told me, "You're up to your armpits in alligators. So tell me, who do you want on your team?"

I looked for proven financial talent anywhere in PepsiCo. There were time constraints. I needed people who could run with the ball, who had the leadership and analytical and financial skills required to operate successfully in crisis mode.

One of the first things I did was to build forecasting and performance tracking systems. I hired an outside consultant to build simple ones on the fly.

The personnel department gave me a list of the people they qualified as financial talent. Larry Bouts had an MBA from Wharton, along with the work ethic and the street smarts to do the job. He had been an officer in the Navy. He was a no-nonsense type of guy, right to the point, and able to carry a heavy load—exactly the kind of person I needed on the team. I made Larry my chief of staff and head of strategy.

We were responsible for fifteen to twenty business units all over the world—Canada, Japan, Belgium, Brazil, Germany, and the Philippines, to name just a few. Larry Bouts recommended that we invite Larry Meyer to join the team because of his transactional expertise. He would be a valuable addition to the team because we planned to sell some of the international units. I called a personal friend who knew Larry Meyer to get his input.

"Len, I'll tell you about Larry," he said. "Don't let his youthful appearance fool you. He's very smart and business savvy, with an incredible work ethic."

Based on what I knew about Larry and my friend's recommendation, I invited him for an interview. Despite his youthful looks, he impressed me. He told me, "Mr. Schutzman, I get things done, and I'm very smart, too. If you select me to be part of your team, I'll do whatever it takes to get the job done." And he kept his word. He became one of the financial managers who led the business planning effort.

From my Corporate Controller's staff, I selected the brightest financial analyst, Tim Kahn, to head up the financial analysis and forecasting processes.

PepsiCo's Treasury function contributed an experienced banker who became one of two new Regional Financial Directors. From the International Franchise division, John Wallace joined the team as Finance Director of the Spanish bottling unit. The Mexico bottling unit was the biggest mess, which is why we brought in two of the strongest people to head up the financial function in Mexico City: Ruben Pietro Paulo and Oswaldo Banos. They were both Argentines, well-trained accountants, and excellent financial managers.

The team worked very hard under very difficult circumstances to get to the bottom of the mess and put the necessary controls in place. Throughout the course of this difficult assignment, we became very close, as they called me frequently to update me about what was going on.

From the transportation division, Bob Thompson joined us as Finance Director in Puerto Rico to straighten out the manipulated books.

Japan was a particularly big mess and I needed a leader for this transformational job. We were losing money while Coca Cola was doing well in that country. I interviewed Don Blair, who was working at the planning department at the time. I liked two things about him: He had a good skill set, and he exuded confidence. I told him, "Don, I need you to move to Japan and be the financial director." He was willing to move, and he stayed in Japan for about six months.

Brazil was another mess where the accounting records had been falsified. Since we needed someone who understood the culture and spoke Portuguese fluently, we hired a recruiting agency to help us find the right person. When they found a suitable candidate, I flew to Brazil to meet him. Miguel Calado had the accounting skills, but I wasn't sure if he had the business acumen, so I took him back to New York with me to give him the right training and meet the rest of the team. As it turned out, he was very good. He was well-versed in U.S. accounting standards and was an excellent businessperson. He showed a lot of potential, and we thought he could grow in PepsiCo. He cleaned up Brazil and became a key member of the management team.

Within a very short period of time, an entirely new division management team was put in place, staffed with the necessary functional expertise and led by the irreverent and outspoken Tom Rattigan, a brilliant and accomplished executive in Pepsi Cola's International Franchise organization. The other members of the senior management team were long-time PepsiCo employees with the needed expertise in personnel, such as John Pearl and John Fulkerson. There was also Phil Ellington (a long-time manufacturing and operations expert from Frito-Lay), and Nestor Carbonell (to handle the sensitive government relationship activities). We retained international controller Marvin Spindler and brought in Rob Barber from corporate to steer up the accounting and financial reporting processes.

The team bonded quickly and began to systematically attack each of the problem areas. While PepsiCo had the financial strength to handle the large accounting write-off, the damage to our image as a great company was significant. In both Mexico and the Philippines, Pepsi Cola was a high-profile business. The scandal and firings were widely covered in the local media. The newly appointed expat management and other PepsiCo management personnel received threats from unhappy terminated employees and outside collaborators. In one case, the new general manager of the Mexico City bottling unit was grabbed and roughed up by thugs.

From that point on, all expat managers were given added security at their offices and residences, with armed drivers and cars to transport them. When anyone from division or corporate headquarters in the U.S. visited these countries, private security guards would meet us at the airport and wouldn't leave our sides until we were safely on the flight home. This was not what I had bargained for when I became a CPA or joined PepsiCo. But we all understood that this was a job that needed to be done, and we were the best team to do it.

A Time for Introspection

At the time, the scandal was one of the biggest instances of fraudulent accounting at a major company to date. Without question, achieving aggressive targets and forecasts was a high priority in PepsiCo's high-performance culture, but we also had a strong code of conduct. A strong culture of ethics and honesty must be the foundation on which any company, of any size, rests.

So, why did it happen? Was there too much pressure on division presidents, causing them to manipulate the results? Was our pay-for-performance compensation system a factor? As we looked for causes, our egos were shattered.

In the Philippines, you don't get your mail delivered without paying someone. Everyone is bribed. Could we still employ non-U.S. financial managers and controllers in emerging markets, where ethical business standards and accounting practices are often not as strong as in the U.S.? Or should we replace everyone who was not American in the financial department? There was tremendous introspection on our part.

In retrospect, this crisis was of great value to the company. Although it caused us a lot of headache and embarrassment, it also helped us to correct course and do our jobs better as time progressed. Hubris can be dangerous, both to individuals and organizations, and a crisis can sometimes be a healthy corrective to those attitudes. By showing us how to do business better in the future, it helped us to become proactive in avoiding the same mistakes.

This International Bottling scandal was definitely the catalyst to re-balance the relationship between performance and our controls and standards. We concluded that it was good to be a high-performance company, but we had to make tweaks. We continued to hire international people and maintained PepsiCo's commitment to attracting and developing the most talented local managers, as we had done with Miguel Calado in Brazil, as long as they understood the American accounting system and agreed to honor PepsiCo's Code of Conduct. Promising local financial managers would be trained in New York by PepsiCo's worldwide internal audit staff. This would not only allow them to learn from similar operations in other countries but would also allow our audit managers to evaluate them.

We had financial controls and policies about how things were supposed to be done. But a central problem in the international units was that their financial people were reporting to the operating guys. While the financial managers were expected to ensure that results were achieved in accordance with generally accepted accounting principles and PepsiCo's Code of Conduct, their recommendations could easily be ignored if they were reporting to the president or unit general manager. This made it hard for us at headquarters in New York to control what was going on.

We made the financial guys responsible for the financial statements. The finance director and controller of each unit were formally given the responsibility to contact senior management and the corporate controller at PepsiCo headquarters if there was any circumventing of proper accounting. We made it clear that although they were working for the local team, they had a stronger responsibility to the corporate office to ensure their numbers were accurate.

PepsiCo Chairman Don Kendall also mandated that appointments of financial executives anywhere in the world had to be approved by Bob Carleton, the corporate controller. Nobody should be paid a bonus without approval from the corporate controller. By putting better controls and higher standards in place, coupled with external involvement in hiring and firing decisions, we reset the bar for international performance. This represented a major step forward in improving the internal control environment.

The fraudulent financial statements had masked business problems at many bottling units. Once we had the accurate statements, my team and I were able to accurately evaluate the options for tackling those business problems.

Coca Cola had a strong market presence, better infrastructure, and strong franchisees in virtually all of the affected countries, which limited viable alternatives. In some countries, Coke outsold us ten to one. When you have a weak market position and you're not making money, it's hard to find a buyer. In some countries, there was no future for Pepsi franchises, and, as we couldn't find a buyer, we had no choice but to close down the businesses. We had to be creative. Based on the poor operating results, we came to the conclusion that in some countries franchising to local businessmen would be the best solution. In a few cases, PepsiCo contributed the assets for a minority stake in the newly combined entity.

When the last international bottling plant was officially sold, we had a private celebration at the corporate office. Each of the outstanding individuals recruited for this unique assignment had made huge sacrifices to clean up the mess. Most of us had traveled extensively, which had taken a toll on us and our families. For the better part of a year, I had lived on airplanes, logging over one million frequent flyer miles as I journeyed to Mexico, Brazil, Spain, Japan, and the Philippines.

A Job Well Done

At our celebration, PepsiCo's CFO walked in the door just as Tom Rattigan, president of the international division, was offering a toast.

"Guys, first of all, I want to thank you for your hard work," Tom said. "Thank you for your commitment and the many, many, many hours you were willing to put in to correct the books and fix the damage. I know it was not an easy assignment. It required you to stretch and perform outside your comfort zones. In a crisis, you get to see what people are really made of. We threw you into the deep, yet you survived and did extraordinarily well. I'm very proud of you. Cheers!"

"Cheers!"

"Cheers!"

Everyone was content that the job was done—and done well.

"It has been quite an adventure," Oswaldo Banos added. "This wasn't like any of the other expat jobs I've had. I never thought I would experience what it would be like to be a celebrity, being escorted by security 24/7."

We all laughed. None of us had anticipated the threats we had received. We were grateful nothing had happened and it was all behind us. Working together so closely under such demanding circumstances had bonded us as a team.

"This is a major accomplishment and a validation for each one of you," I said. "We completed Mission Impossible, and I'd like to toast to that."

As a result of our efforts, PepsiCo no longer had company-owned bottling plants outside of North America. But once our initial "mission" was completed, we received the assignment to expand Pepsi Cola to China and other emerging markets. Coca Cola had a strong position in the developed countries, so we wanted to focus on countries where there was a level playing field, like India and China.

Cleaning up the mess in Pepsi Bottling International was like providing life support to a dying patient; but now my involvement in Pepsi Cola International promised to be more fun because we would have the opportunity to build and grow.

STEP #3. TAKEAWAYS!

Every business, from time to time, hits a patch of rough waters and has problems. Properly addressing these problems should always be a top priority for the business unit operating management, the senior corporate executives, and the board of directors. Occasionally, cross-functional corporate staff teams are formed in an effort to provide a fresh point of view on the underlying problems the company faces. If management changes are necessary, your involvement on these study teams can place you in a strong position for a promotional opportunity.

Businesses that are in trouble cause a major headache for all the top people in the company and the board of directors, so anyone who can positively contribute to resolving the problem has a chance to receive a lot of recognition. Most people want to stay away from problems and businesses that are losing money, but if you can make a positive impact, your efforts will be rewarded.

Driving a car on a straightaway is pretty easy compared to driving on a race track, where you need to make a lot of turns and course corrections. One of the reasons that these people developed so quickly is that they were thrown in over their heads and given the chance to take risks. If you can make an impact in a business that's in trouble, it demonstrates a different kind of skill set. Most of all, making meaningful contributions to any turnaround situation will raise your profile as a fast-tracker.

Some people on the crisis team we assembled were concerned that being involved in cleaning up the international bottling scandal would cast a black mark on their careers, but the opposite was the case. This involvement accelerated their development. Going through the crisis separated the boys from the men. They had picked up so much experience that executives from other big corporations were hunting for them and offered them high-level positions that doubled their current salaries. Although PepsiCo wanted to retain the team and find them the right jobs within the corporation, not everybody stayed. Those who stayed were consolidated in Pepsi Cola International, and I became the CFO.

Here's how you can put Step Three into operation:

Takeaway No. 1: Become involved in a turnaround situation, because it will raise your profile. Every business occasionally goes through difficult periods, and special cross-functional task forces are created to bring fresh eyes to address these challenges. To the extent that you can get involved in these situations and be seen as a contributor to the solution, you can significantly enhance your reputation and propel your career.

Takeaway No. 2: In a crisis, develop an action plan. After we confirmed the fraud we suspected, many important steps had to be taken. The SEC had to be informed and a press release sent out to inform the public. The next steps were to replace anyone involved in the cover-up and figure out how to rebuild the companies. Confronted by a crisis, a detailed action plan is a necessity.

Takeaway No. 3: When in crisis mode, act with speed. Speed is of the essence when handling a crisis because events are unfolding rapidly and you have to get on top of them as soon as possible. Delay and indecision will only make the problem worse and create the impression that the company is not engaged with the crisis.

Takeaway No. 4: While acting with speed, assemble a crisis team carefully. In a crisis, make sure to select the key people, but don't spread the team too thin. I carefully selected my crisis team to deal with the international bottling crisis. I looked for those people who had the expertise, character, and specific skills to address the complex problems we faced.

Takeaway No. 5: A crisis can be a necessary antidote for hubris. While the international bottling scandal was a nightmare for PepsiCo, it also helped us identify ways to improve the ways we did business. The scandal exposed flaws in our decision-making and controls. The resulting introspection made us a much better and more tightly managed company.

Takeaway No. 6: Dealing with a crisis will accelerate the development of key executives. Some people on the crisis team thought their involvement in the international bottling scandal would cast a black mark on their careers, but their involvement accelerated their development. They had picked up so much experience that executives from other big corporations were hunting for them and offered them high-level positions that doubled their salaries. The same can happen to you.

The Next Step!

What I learned from my experience in the international bottling scandal was the importance of integrity above all else. When you have integrity, you're able to operate from a solid foundation that will guide all your other actions. My belief in integrity was further strengthened during the next stage in my career when I faced a crisis in one of PepsiCo's major divisions. My faith in Step Four was strengthened even more—to fast-track your career, you must have integrity above everything else.

CHAPTER FIVE

STEP #4. INTEGRITY ABOVE ALL ELSE

When I say that integrity is the bedrock quality for any senior executive, I mean it, because I learned its importance the hard way—first, during the international bottling scandal, and a second time at Frito-Lay. I learned during my career that integrity means objectively providing the facts and "telling it like it is" without sugarcoating, no matter what the consequences might be. When you have integrity above all else, people will have confidence in you. It's the foundation for any successful career. In fact, without it, you won't have any career at all.

Let's take a look at how I continued to learn the lessons of Step Four during my career. . . .

One day in 1986, opportunity came knocking again. I received a call from Wayne Calloway, PepsiCo's CEO. We had known each other for many years, but his call came as a surprise.

"Hey Len, how are you?"

"I'm great, Wayne. How have you been?"

"I know you're curious about the reason for my call," Wayne said, as if he were reading my mind. "We're looking for a CFO for Frito-Lay. No one has as much experience as you do in the different business units, and, if you're interested, I think you'll be the perfect candidate for the job."

"Thank you so much for thinking of me. That certainly is a great position. I'm flattered."

In truth, I had mixed feelings about the offer. Frito-Lay was PepsiCo's largest and most profitable business unit, and being asked to be the CFO was a plum assignment by any standard. But it would require my family to move again, this time to Texas, and the last move to California had not proven to be very successful.

"I appreciate your call, Wayne, but before I can give you my answer I'll have to talk with my family first."

"Not a problem. Just give me a call."

I had only been with Pepsi Cola International for less than a year, and now this huge opportunity presented itself. Frito-Lay was PepsiCo's most important business. Because it would add to my experience in the restaurant industry and the expertise I had gained in international business, becoming Frito-Lay's CFO would allow me to me to further strengthen my background. It could position me to one day become the CFO of PepsiCo.

That day, I went home early, so I could talk to my wife and children. After explaining that the job offer was a huge opportunity and would not require as much travel as working for Pepsi Cola International, they agreed to support my career and move to Texas. We flew in the private company plane to Dallas. We spent a day looking for houses and eventually found a nice one in Plano. We sold our home in Connecticut and once again packed our belongings, said goodbye to our friends and family, and left behind the world we knew.

I loved the opportunity. Being in a stable business like Frito-Lay would be a welcome change from the turbulent three years I had spent cleaning up the International Bottling division. But I was in for a surprise.

Frito-Lay normally produced consistently high-profit growth, but I noticed that performance was waning. My initial observation determined that there were several factors contributing to this problem. The new President had made the decision to expand Frito-Lay's market from salty snacks to include sweet and savory snacks.

A Problem with the Numbers

These products were very different from Frito-Lay's core business. They had slower category growth, lower margins, different competitors, and required significant capital investment in new manufacturing facilities. Because we had to divert marketing funds and our salespeople's focus to these new products, sales of the core salty snack business were negatively affected. On top of that, route trucks were carrying these lower margin products instead of the higher margin salty snacks. My initial meetings with the president and his senior staff confirmed my worst fears: They were living in their own dream world. They refused to acknowledge the current situation and were sending increasingly unrealistic financial forecasts to PepsiCo.

As the financial person, I knew it was my responsibility to have high integrity and a degree of healthy skepticism. Someone had to play the role of the devil's advocate—and as the CFO, that was my role. At the same time, I had very little experience in the company, having joined them only a few weeks earlier. To strengthen the finance leadership team, I asked Jerry Martin, a long-time Frito-Lay employee with prior experience in planning and operations, to rejoin the group as Vice President of Business Planning. Jerry's organizational knowledge and relationships within the company provided me with important credibility, and using trend analysis, I built a new financial model for forecasting.

Integrity is an essential characteristic that every successful executive must possess. For a financial person, integrity means providing a fair and balanced evaluation and always telling it like it is, sticking to the facts and not sugarcoating anything. People need to have confidence in what you're saying.

So I called Bob Dettmer, as he was my functional boss, and told him, "Bob, I've only been at Frito-Lay for a few weeks, but you know I'm not a rookie. The forecasts PepsiCo is receiving are a fairy tale. There are two people deep in the organization who validate my assessment. What do you suggest I do?"

Bob sounded concerned. "This is a pretty serious accusation, Len. How sure are you about this?"

"I don't know for sure," I replied in complete honesty. "Nothing is for sure, but I'm pretty sure that I'm right."

"Why don't you give it a little more time to see if your observation really is correct?" Bob asked.

"Bob, I know that the CEO is very close to Wayne Calloway, and that does not put me in a good position. But I can't put it on the back burner and wait another month. Things will only get worse. I have to talk to Wayne—I owe it to him. I'll show him the presentation. He knows the business well. He'll be able to tell if I'm right."

"Okay, Len," Bob said. "You have to do the right thing. I'll do my best to protect you, but you'd better be right."

"Thanks, Bob. I'll see you soon." I hung up the phone.

It was a difficult situation, but I knew I had to do it. I finished the presentation I had prepared for Wayne and decided to show it to the CEO of Frito-Lay. I figured that if it was off-base, he would tell me.

Accompanied by several of my staff members, I met with Frito-Lay's CEO. I explained to him, "We are very much concerned about the state of the business and what you're telling Pepsi about it. If you keep going this way, we're headed for trouble."

I showed him the presentation we had put together, but he refused to even look at it.

"This is a pile of shit!" he yelled and tossed it aside. The CEO told me, "Len, you're not a marketing guy. You don't know what you're doing. You're just a numbers guy."

I was so mad that I walked out the room and slammed the door. My team came running after me.

Telling It Like It Is

Despite what I considered to be overwhelming evidence, the CEO refused to alter his strategy or modify the forecasts.

I had a big problem. The CEO was very well liked by Wayne Calloway, PepsiCo's CEO; Wayne had put him in that position. But there was not much soul-searching on my part—I knew what integrity meant and what a financial person had to do. Pepsi was getting an Alice in Wonderland view, and I needed to correct it.

I was a little nervous that my actions might be premature, because I had been at Frito-Lay for just a few weeks. But if I was wrong, the worst thing that could happen was that I'd get fired. And if I was right, I could also get fired. Either way, I knew that I had to bring this information to PepsiCo's attention.

I got on a plane to New York to meet with Wayne Calloway and Bob Dettmer, PepsiCo's CFO, to brief them on what was happening at Frito-Lay. Frito-Lay was the most successful business Pepsi had ever added and consistently delivered unbelievable earnings. To summarize the importance of Frito-Lay to PepsiCo's overall performance, it was said that when Frito-Lay sneezed, PepsiCo caught a cold.

"Good to see you, Len," Wayne said, welcoming me. "How's your family? Are they getting adjusted to life in Texas?"

"We're still settling in," I said. "The culture is very different from Connecticut."

We chatted for a few minutes until Bob joined us. As soon as he closed the door behind him, I said, "Wayne, I have some very disturbing news about Frito-Lay."

That, of course, was the last thing Wayne was expecting to hear.

"Frito-Lay is the crown jewel of PepsiCo," he said. "How can that be?"

As Wayne and Bob listened closely, I explained.

"Potato chips, pretzels, and other salty snacks have been Frito-Lay's core business for many years," I said. "But there's been a recent shift in the product line to sweet snacks like cookies and more dessert-like products. That is not the business that has brought Frito-Lay success. The CEO is telling the sales team to sell the sweet products, and if there's not enough space on the truck to bring both, the core salty products are left behind. Sales are down because they are cannibalizing our core products. There is no way that the projections they have been giving you are going to be matched. They are way off the map, and I can show you our analysis."

Wayne was speechless as I presented him the numbers.

"Wayne," I continued, "I know you're close to the President of Frito-Lay. I understand it's not an easy decision. What I've learned from you and Bob is that it's my responsibility as the financial guy to tell the truth and let you know what's going on. It would be easy to sugarcoat the situation, but we've seen what that led to during the international fiasco. I'm telling you, Frito-Lay is a locomotive out of control, and I'm very fearful about where it's headed."

Wayne was shocked about what was happening in Dallas. He took a minute and then said, "I have to think about it. Will you be around?"

"I'll be here," I responded. "I'm not going back to Dallas until you've decided what you're going to do."

As we walked to the car together, Bob said, "Don't worry, Len. Wayne is known for his integrity. Let's wait to hear what he says."

"Well," I responded as I got in the car, "if I have to go back to Dallas, you had better give me an armed guard."

The Right Decision

I was spending time with old friends in New York after the meeting when my cell phone rang. It was Wayne.

"I see what you're talking about," he said, "and I need to make a move. I'm going to move Michael Jordan in. He's one of the highest senior executives with experience in Frito-Lay, and the two of you will be responsible for getting the company back on the right track. I wish the CEO had told me what was going on sooner. Now, I have no other choice but to replace him and bring in a new CEO. Michael is known and respected in Dallas, and you have a good staff, so I have full confidence that the two of you will fix this before it's too late. Please talk to Michael, so you can get started at the beginning of next week."

"Thank you, Wayne," I said in relief. "That wasn't an easy decision."

"You did the right thing, Len."

I had made the right decision—and I still had my job!

Michael and I put together a plan to refocus on core salty snack growth and exit the other product lines that were a distraction to this strategy. Charlie

Feld was Frito-Lay's Vice President of Management Information Systems. Charlie was a forward-thinking technologist, the prime mover in Frito-Lay's pioneering development of handheld computer devices that allowed route salesmen to prepare sales invoices, as well as input information directly into the accounting systems. Charlie was also an astute business thinker. In the turnaround effort, Michael and I frequently sought out Charlie's insights and opinions on strategic shifts.

Charley's role as a leading IT thinker was recognized in the industry, with *Forbes* magazine calling him, "The Greatest CIO for Hire in History." He was also among the first inductees into *CIO Magazine*'s CIO Hall of Fame.

But what I remember most is his thoughtful counsel on the possible risks in evaluating alternative strategies. As we implemented the new strategies to save Frito-Lay, Charlie and the business planning team put meaningful new reporting in place to monitor performance.

STEP #4. TAKEAWAYS!

It isn't easy to have integrity. There are many ways we can take shortcuts or look the other way. But if we take that route, we're endangering our businesses, our customers, and our careers. Only by putting integrity front and center can we build a solid foundation for successful businesses and successful careers.

Here are the key steps you can take to bring integrity to your work:

Takeaway No. 1: Always have a degree of healthy skepticism. Healthy skepticism means that you never take anything at face value. Someone has to play the role of the devil's advocate in order to challenge assumptions and ways of doing business that may be harmful to the company. This was my approach when the numbers at Frito-Lay didn't add up.

Takeaway No. 2: Stick to the facts, always tell it like it is, and never sugarcoat anything. Integrity is a bedrock quality for any senior executive. It means objectively providing the facts and "telling it like it is" without sugarcoating, no matter what the consequences might be. This is particularly true for financial managers. Without this kind of transparency, a corporation will be on the road toward a potential crisis.

Takeaway No. 3: Don't let personal relationships interfere with your objectivity. As a healthy skeptic, you need to have the courage and fortitude to overlook personal relationships. You have to let the chips fall where they may, in an objective manner, even if it means putting the spotlight on those who are close to you in the organization or who have a close relationship with high-ranking people.

The Next Step!

Michael and I had spent eight months analyzing the challenges, laying out the business, and creating the plan to get Frito-Lay back on track. We were still fully engaged in executing the plan when a new door of opportunity opened up for me that was completely unexpected but that I was fully prepared to embrace. That's because I had known all along about the importance of Step Five—getting involved in acquisitions—in turbo-charging one's corporate career.

Chapter Six

Step #5. Get Involved in Acquisitions

If you can contribute to special projects in high visibility areas, such as acquisitions and international business development, you can shine in the eyes of senior management and propel your career to new heights. That's what happened to me at age thirty-two, when I was involved in the Taco Bell acquisition. In the years since, I had kept my eyes open for new acquisition possibilities where I could use my talents to the fullest. I was always ready to put Step Five into action.

The opportunity came one January day in 1987, when Bob Dettmer called me. Even though I had been in different positions over the years, Bob, who had been my functional boss in the past, had stayed in close contact. He was known for his leadership, and I valued his friendship. I thought he was getting in touch to find out how things were going at Frito-Lay.

After briefly discussing what was happening in the division, Bob said, "Len, I have exciting news for you. The position of Senior Vice President and Treasurer opened up at PepsiCo corporate, and I arranged for you to get this position—if you're interested, of course."

A Great New Opportunity

I was pleasantly surprised. Michael Jordan, the CEO of Frito-Lay, and I had spent the last eight months working on the plan that would get Frito-Lay back on track. We had barely started with the implementation, and here I was being presented this great new opportunity.

"Thank you for thinking of me, Bob," I said with a smile on my face. "That sounds like a great promotion, and I'll be able to move back to New York."

"With your merchants and acquisition experience, as well as your international experience, you would be perfect for the job," Bob replied. "You have a broad experience in PepsiCo, and I'm confident you'll do a great job. What we need from you is to make some big acquisitions at the corporate office. We're looking at major international acquisitions. So, are you in?"

"Absolutely! I'll have to talk with Michael to see when I can make the transition. I want to make sure that we have someone to replace me before I leave."

Bob was agreeable to this. "I understand. Knowing your level of responsibility and integrity, I hadn't expected anything else. You always have the best interests of everyone in mind, and that's a great quality."

When the call ended, I walked over to the window. There was still a lot that had to be accomplished to get Frito-Lay to its previous level of profitability. I wouldn't be there to finish the project, and yet I knew that I had made my contribution. Being the Treasurer of PepsiCo would be an exciting new challenge. It didn't happen by coincidence, though. I had very carefully deployed the Eight Steps to fast-track the corporate ladder—and with great success.

As I looked outside, I contemplated my years at PepsiCo. When I was offered a job with the company eleven years earlier, I somehow had known that it would allow me to gain a broader perspective than staying at the firm where I had been working. Others thought I was crazy to leave a position where I was on track to becoming a partner, but I knew I had made the right decision. If I had not made the jump, I would have still been a bean counter. Instead, I had the opportunity to become the CFO of Taco Bell, clean up PepsiCo's international bottling crisis, and work closely with Michael, the CEO of Frito-Lay, to develop plans that would ensure the division's future growth. I would not have wanted to miss any of these experiences.

A knock on the door brought me out of my thoughts. "Yes?" I said, caught a little off guard.

"Len, congratulations!"

It was Michael Jordan, wearing a bright smile. I was glad to see his smile, because I felt I was leaving him behind in a project we started together.

"I've heard the exciting news," he continued, "and I wanted to make sure to be the first one to congratulate you. Of course we'll miss you at Frito-Lay, but I'm happy for you. It's a dream job. And I have a feeling we'll still be working together, as you'll be responsible for acquisitions."

"Thank you, Michael, I appreciate it. It's a really nice promotion, and I'm looking forward to it."

"I know they want you to come to New York as soon as possible," Michael said as he sat down, "so we'll need to find your successor right away. You know all the financial people. Who would be the best person? Anyone come to mind?"

After giving it some thought and going through my rolodex, I said, "There are three people who qualify to take over my role. Each of them will be a great asset in helping you execute the plan that we created together successfully."

Michael and I discussed the pros and cons of each person and agreed to start the interview process as soon as I had talked with Wayne Calloway and Bob Dettmer.

I helped Michael find the right guy to replace me as the new CFO of Frito-Lay. I recommended Dave Rader, one of the many successful fast-trackers I had mentored over the last few years. He had been an engineer for Ford. When I first met him, he was working as an analyst. He told me, "Len, I don't want to be just an analyst. I want to be a manager and make things happen." I knew he was a fast-tracker with much potential. I decided to mentor him and help him achieve his career goals.

When I became the CFO of Taco Bell, I hired David as the vice president of financial planning and strategy, and he later became the controller. In my opinion, David was the best person for the job. I knew he was a quick study and had great financial skills. He was soft-spoken but high-impact. He had the skills and the perfect temperament. But Michael wasn't convinced that he had enough experience, and he selected someone else to succeed me.

Two years later, Michael named David as CFO of Frito-Lay, and he stayed there for ten years until he retired. He was considered the best of the best by his peers for the impact he had. Within PepsiCo, David was considered the gold standard for a CFO.

The Smiths and Walkers Acquisition

As PepsiCo's Treasurer, I was responsible for acquisitions, risk management, worldwide financing, capital management and investments, and taxes, and I would be closely working with bankers, shareholders, and investors. I had some experience with acquisitions and foreign exchange, but the rest was new to me. Despite my lack of experience in certain areas, I was able to hit the ground running because of my experience with acquisitions and because I had great resources in my network. Five or six guys knew everything I needed to know. They helped me understand my new role and introduced me to others. I built my Treasury team. I had to bolster up the Merchant and Acquisition side of the business, so I hired John Kale, an experienced deal maker, and Tom Davin from Goldman Sachs as assistant treasurers.

Even though I had left Frito-Lay in the day-to-day, Michael Jordan made me promise to look at acquisition opportunities for Frito-Lay outside the U.S. So I continued to be involved with that division, working on strategic international acquisitions. PepsiCo's primary interest was to acquire Smiths and Walkers Crisps, a leading U.K. snack company owned by RJR Nabisco, the global consumer products company. A private equity firm had taken on debt to take on RJR Nabisco. Most analysts and media commentators assumed that they might divest of non-core businesses to pay down some of the debt.

I made our interest known to RJR Nabisco's investment bankers, and they told me that they would get back with me after the transition closed. A few days later, on June 6, my assistant ran into my office and handed me a press release stating that French biscuit company BSN had entered into an agreement to acquire the European biscuit division of RJR Nabisco, which included

Smiths and Walkers Crisps.

We had no idea that a divestiture of this sort was in the works. But when I informed my bosses of what had taken place, I reminded them that "it's not over until the fat lady sings."

They said, "How can you say it's not over?"

"I have an idea," I told them. "I have done my homework."

I knew that the purchase price of $2.5 billion would require BSN to incur significant borrowings and drive up their leverage ratio to unusually high levels. It was known that BSN was primarily interested in the European biscuit businesses and would consider selling off the other companies in the future.

I called the investment bankers and told them, "You blind-sided me. Do you know where Mr. Riboud is staying? I need to talk to him personally." They told me he was at the Waldorf Astoria Hotel in New York.

I had never met the BSN Chairman, Monsieur Riboud. Nevertheless, I decided to put a call in to him to see if there was a possibility of a mutually beneficial transaction. When I called the hotel, I was transferred to his room, and he answered the phone.

"Congratulations, Monsieur Riboud," I said. "You've handled the purchase very skillfully."

"Thank you, Mr. Schutzman, we are very delighted with the acquisition," Monsieur Riboud responded, obviously curious for the reason of my call.

"Monsieur Riboud, PepsiCo is interested in acquiring Smiths and Walkers. There are many advantages for BSN to do this transaction with us soon. I would like to meet with you."

Monsieur Riboud responded, "My flight to Paris leaves in a few hours, Mr. Schutzman."

"Michael Jordan, the President of Frito-Lay, and I can meet you in Paris tomorrow at noon," I said, believing in the merits of moving quickly.

"Well, tomorrow is a bit soon," Monsieur Riboud responded. "Why don't you schedule a time with my assistant for the end of next week? That will be much better. I have a lot of press conferences and other things to do this week. I'm very busy, you see."

He was reluctant to schedule a meeting so soon, since they were still basking in their victory, but he eventually agreed to meet with us.

"I'm looking forward to our meeting tomorrow, Monsieur Riboud," I told him.

Before he hung up the phone, he warned me: "But don't get your hopes up. We're not going to sell unless we receive top dollar. You can meet me in Paris, but I can't give you any guarantees."

Playing Hardball

Michael and I got on the corporate Concorde to Paris and arrived the next morning. We checked in at the hotel and took a taxi to Mr. Riboud's office. According to our analysis, $1.35 billion would represent a fair price for Smiths and Walkers.

After exchanging pleasantries, Mr. Riboud began the meeting by stating, "I appreciate your visit, but I hope that your trip has not been made in vain. We're not interested in selling part of the business we just acquired, but if the price is right, we may be willing to part with Smiths and Walkers Crisps. And when I say if the price is right, I'm thinking that $1.8 billion would be a good price for Smiths and Walkers."

I responded briefly with comments on the valuation of these businesses. Michael then went over our strategic thinking and options and said, "In most markets we have successfully greenfielded new snack businesses using our stable of global snack food brand leaders, and we are prepared to do this in England if we can't reach a deal. PepsiCo has the resources and the expertise to start a brand new company, in which case we'll become your competitor. And since PepsiCo is a conglomerate that very few companies will likely want to compete with, it will scare some buyers away, and the rest won't be willing to pay as much."

"If you sell Smiths and Walkers to us, you'll look even smarter," I continued. "You will have what you wanted for a great price."

Based on my extensive analysis, I explained the numbers to him. Riboud could tell we had done our homework. We were an obvious player, and he knew we had the money. If they were to sell Smiths and Walkers for $1.3 billion, their net acquisition cost for the biscuit businesses (which was their primary interest) would be $1.2 billion, a remarkably low multiple of the earnings of those businesses, and, further, it would eliminate the need to burden their balance sheet with new debt. I wanted to show him that we were paying a fair price.

My objective was to move in and scoop it up now. Waiting would have been to his advantage, not to ours. His investment banker would suggest a competitive auction, and Kellogg's and other companies might have been interested. That wasn't what I wanted.

"Everybody will be praising you for this deal," I continued. "If you don't sell, you'll have to borrow billions of dollars, and there is no guarantee that anybody is going to buy for a higher price, especially when they hear that they'll be competing with Frito-Lay."

Mr. Riboud knew that I made some good points. Not particularly happy, he suggested that we take a fifteen-minute break.

"That's a good idea," I said. "That will allow me the time to confer with my superiors in New York."

Michael and I talked privately about whether we should raise our offer. I said we should stick to our guns.

"Let's go to $1.4 billion," Michael suggested. He really wanted to close the deal, but I felt there was a better chance we would win. We could have lost the deal, but I was willing to take the risk.

"If we raise the offer, then he'll think we have more money to spend," I replied. I was sure we had to play hardball. Michael finally agreed not to raise the price.

When the meeting reconvened, Mr. Riboud asked, "Gentlemen, are you willing to increase your bid? That way, a quick deal can be achieved."

Michael looked at me, knowing that we had more negotiation space, but I remained firm and said, "Mr. Riboud, we can close the deal before you close the deal, and you won't have to borrow the money for your acquisition. This is our last offer. I'm ready to fly back to New York. Do you accept it or not?"

Hesitantly, he asked, "Can you close the deal in two weeks?"

This would be simultaneous with their RJR Nabisco closing. I could hardly contain myself. I knew we had won. When Michael answered, "Yes, we can," Mr. Riboud extended his hand and said, "We have a deal." We shook hands.

As we got into the cab, Michael scolded me, "Len, did you really have to be so hard-nosed? We probably could have justified another $50 million."

I smiled. "I had a feeling that they weren't ready to let us leave. Why spend the money if we didn't have to?"

"You certainly convinced them that we were willing to walk away," Michael replied. "I could hardly believe it."

I laughed. "When I walked down the hall to the restroom earlier, I had noticed a room set up with bottles of champagne on ice. If I had not seen the champagne, I might not have been as bold. You have to keep your eyes open for the indicators of where people are in any negotiation. My deal teacher, former PepsiCo CFO Herman Schaeffer, once told me, 'Until they're convinced that you're willing to walk away, you can't negotiate the best deal.' That sage advice has remained an integral part of my approach to negotiations."

It was no wonder PepsiCo's former Chairman, Wayne Calloway, used to say, "Len Schutzman is our best deal negotiator because he's not afraid to walk away."

Michael said, "Your strategy worked, Len! Congratulations!"

We had gone from the depths of despair twenty-four hours earlier, when we heard that someone else had purchased the snack businesses we coveted, to today's handshake deal on acquiring Smiths and Walkers.

"Today showed that it's not over until the fat lady sings," I said.

Michael and I took the Concorde back to New York to celebrate our victory with the rest of the executive team.

The Gamesa Acquisition

As Smiths and Walker grew rapidly and became a stronger division within our brand, Michael began looking for ways to continue the international expansion. When we talked a few months later, he asked me, "What are some other big companies that we can acquire?"

I told Michael that I had just heard from one of my contacts that there might be an opportunity opening up. "One of the people in my network, Violy McCausland, told me that Gamesa, one of the biggest food companies in Mexico, might be willing to sell. It's complicated because it's a family business, but let me see what I can do."

Gamesa was owned by a mother and her four children. When a family is involved, emotions play a bigger role than money in the decision-making process around a possible sale. Luckily, Violy knew the family personally, and her insight in what was going on behind the scenes provided us with invaluable information that allowed us to close the deal.

After talking to the mother, Violy realized that she wanted to keep the business as a family legacy to honor her late husband, whereas each child had a different view about a possible transaction. The oldest son was a senator, and he thought it would look bad if a prestigious Mexican company was sold to an American company. He was concerned about maintaining the family's favorable reputation and avoiding adverse public opinion. Other sons wanted to sell the business and cash out.

Violy was able to guide us during the deal. She understood the family and worked with us to find out what would motivate them to sell to PepsiCo. Without Violy, we would not have found out this important information.

We explained to the son who opposed the sale that the transaction would create a lot of new jobs in Mexico. We agreed to move R & D there, to help the country's economy. The daughter didn't seem to care much about the money. She was the vote we needed to pull this thing off, but she wasn't willing to cooperate until our advisor discovered that her passion was dance and art, and, in particular, supporting ballet in Mexico. That was her highest priority. Don Kendall, Pepsi's chairman, happened to be a ballet lover. He had brought Baryshnikov to the U.S., so he had a lot of sway with the daughter during our negotiations. We made a commitment that we would support ballet in Mexico and the daughter's dance troupe, and that sealed the deal.

By understanding the emotions and motives of each person involved and by creating a proposal that made each family member happy, PepsiCo was able to close the deal and acquire Gamesa. It was the biggest acquisition ever of a Mexican company.

Taking an American Subsidiary Public in Japan

Another great project took place in Japan, where PepsiCo owned Kentucky Fried Chicken in partnership with Mitsubishi. We had Pizza Hut and Taco Bell at the time, so chicken seemed to be a good addition. Even though KFC was bigger than McDonalds in Japan, it wasn't growing fast. So I asked my team, "What can be done to increase shareholder value?"

One person on our team came up with the idea to take part of the company public on the Tokyo Stock Exchange. I asked Claudia, my assistant treasurer, to research what the value would be to PepsiCo. What would KFC's management team think about it? What would Mitsubishi think about it? What would be the major challenges? What was the probability that we could pull this off? She wrote a white paper that determined it would be very profitable to take part of the company public, as they would get seventy times earnings at the stock offering. However, nobody had ever taken the subsidiary of an American company public in the Japanese stock market.

Claudia and I went to Japan and met with Goldman Sachs in Tokyo. We spent a lot of time in that country building relationships and finding out how we could make it happen. We had Mitsubishi as a partner in Japan, and I had to convince them that they would benefit, too. Because we would be the first to take the subsidiary of an American company public in Japan, it would be good publicity. The Japanese people could own part of KFC. We would only sell 20 percent of the stock, and PepsiCo and Mitsubishi would own the remaining 80 percent. When we promised Mitsubishi that they would get first rights to buy PepsiCo's shares if we decided to sell, they agreed to the deal.

Claudia became the point person on this project, but the Japanese were reluctant to accept orders from a woman. They requested that a male executive be the go-between, rather than dealing with Claudia directly.

My friends from Goldman Sachs told me I was pushing the envelope on this and it may not be a good idea. "Japanese society isn't going to be ready for this," they said.

"Well, I don't know about that," I replied. "I think you've got to stand up for the things you believe in."

And that's what I did. The Japanese told me that I was being culturally insensitive by insisting that a woman be in charge of the deal. I told them that Claudia was very capable and did her job very well; there was no reason to add another person in the middle of negotiations. If they wanted to do business with an American company, they had to value our culture as well. At one point, I told the bankers that I would find another bank if needed. Claudia handled the deal very well, and it was a good experience for the Japanese. With her skilled help, we took a subsidiary of KFC public in Japan, becoming the first company to list the subsidiary of an American company on the Tokyo stock exchange.

Stopping a Bad Deal from Being Made: General Foods (1986-1987)

In putting Step Five into action, sometimes your role is to identify acquisitions that do not meet the corporation's standards, in order to stop a bad deal from being made. Such was the case during my experience as PepsiCo's Treasurer with the potential acquisition of General Foods in 1986-87. I was charged with investigating whether we should make the deal.

When General Foods announced that it was putting itself up for sale, I was inundated with calls from investment bankers who wanted to represent us in a transaction. Many industry experts believed that PepsiCo would be the ideal company to acquire General Foods because our strong position in the food industry and exceptional management team would improve the performance of the General Foods brands. However, many of General Foods' product lines were growing slowly and commodity-like in margins. As a result, many PepsiCo executives were skeptical about whether they could move the needle on those businesses to increase PepsiCo shareholder value.

I didn't have a good feeling about this acquisition from the start because one of General Food's top product lines was coffee, which is a commodity and in a different market from PepsiCo's experience.

I reverse-engineered our acquisition model to calculate the unit volume growth and margin increases necessary to justify the assumed acquisition price. The analysis showed that in order to make it worthwhile, we would have to grow revenues by 2 to 3 percent, so I asked the operating guys if we could increase the margin by that rate. When they told me that it was highly unlikely, I knew it wasn't a deal we should chase. The answer was clear: The acquisition of General Foods at that price could not be justified in terms of shareholder value accretion.

General Foods wasn't a good match with our core businesses. Our growth rates and returns in our core food and beverage businesses were superior to those of General Foods. General Foods had to be fixed, and they didn't necessarily have the expertise to do it. The company had been sold several times before. My advice to PepsiCo's President was that we shouldn't place a bid. I showed him that we would be wasting a lot of time and resources not only in negotiating, but also in fixing the business. It was up to him to make the decision, but that was my advice. This decision reinforced the market's perception of PepsiCo as being savvy and disciplined in its approach to acquisitions. As a result, whatever future acquisitions we did make were viewed positively by the stock market.

In an acquisition scenario, it's easy to get carried away by the hoopla. Every deal has a price. As the financial guy, you have to play tough and be the devil's advocate. That's the cornerstone of being a successful financial person.

Reflections on Acquisitions

When you're putting Step Five into action, it's important to be cautious. As mentioned earlier, there's often a great deal of enthusiasm surrounding the possibility of an acquisition: the excitement of acquiring a new business, possible synergies and enhanced growth prospects for existing businesses, potential job openings, etc.

But it is the responsibility of the company's financial organization to be wary of that enthusiasm by preparing a well-thought-out model, supported by reasonable assumptions, to ensure that the acquisition creates shareholder value.

With all the euphoria and hoopla, it is easy to fall into line and be a team player. Therefore, it's important that the financial executive be disciplined, playing the devil's advocate to ensure that all issues are adequately considered.

The General Foods case discussed earlier provides an excellent example of the constructive role that the financial executive can play in highlighting the magnitude of improvements required to justify an acquisition.

STEP #5. TAKEAWAYS!

A successful acquisition requires cross-functional input from many parts of the company (including accounting, tax, treasury, and legal), and consequently presents you with an excellent opportunity to demonstrate a wide range of skills. By becoming involved in acquisitions, you will position yourself to be recognized and rewarded for your ability to put your diverse set of talents into action.

Here are the specific actions you can take when putting Step Five into action:

Takeaway No. 1: Always do your homework. I knew that the purchase price of $2.5 billion would require BSN to incur significant borrowings and drive up their leverage ratio to unusually high levels. By doing my homework and finding out the key background information, I realized it would be in BSN's best interest to sell Smiths and Walkers, giving us tremendous leverage going into the negotiations.

Takeaway No. 2: Be prepared to move quickly. BSN was reluctant to schedule a meeting so soon, but I pushed them to meet with us as quickly as possible. Had I not done that, PepsiCo may never have acquired Smiths and Walkers.

Takeaway No. 3: Be willing to take the risk by playing hardball. We were prepared to open a business in England to compete with BSN. I was also prepared to walk away from the BSN deal if they didn't accept my offer. Until the other side is convinced you're playing hardball and are willing to walk away if you don't get what you want, you can't close the best possible deal in your favor.

Takeaway No. 4: Keep your eyes open for the indicators of where people are. When I noticed a room set up with bottles of champagne on ice during the BSN deal, it convinced me they were ready to make a deal. If I hadn't seen the champagne, I might not have been as bold in my negotiations. During acquisitions and deal making, look for subtle signs that indicate where the other side is.

Takeaway No. 5: Play the devil's advocate. Playing the "devil's advocate" is never a popular role, but it is a prime responsibility during acquisitions. Always be skeptical. You can get caught up in the excitement, but you have to look hard at the business and the numbers. Make sure all issues and risks are raised and examined, and provide financial modeling and sensitivity analysis to ensure that shareholder value will be created. That's how I was able to convince the president of PepsiCo that acquiring General Foods was not in the company's interest.

Takeaway No. 6: Joint ventures can be better than acquisitions. Joint ventures can be better than acquisitions when the companies can complement one another, creating a win/win situation.

Takeaway No. 7: Know the fundamentals behind any potential acquisition. In an acquisition, companies can have widely different manufacturing processes and forms of distribution. One company may be vulnerable to agricultural conditions and commodity prices; the other may not. It's important to take a deep look at the fundamentals of both companies in any acquisition situation. Without this due diligence, you're operating blind in a very risky situation.

The Next Step!

By now, I had risen to a very high position as Treasurer at PepsiCo. But that didn't stop me from continuing to build relationships, both inside and outside the company, that could help the business and, in turn, help me. No matter where you are in your career, never lose sight of the next step, which is to build strong relationships within your network of contacts.

CHAPTER SEVEN

STEP #6. BUILD STRONG RELATIONSHIPS WITH YOUR NETWORK

Building strong relationships is crucial to fast-tracking your corporate career. Having strong relationships with the right people played a big role in my journey from bean counter to becoming the treasurer of a multi-billion-dollar company. When I was with PepsiCo, I had a network of fifty people, both inside and outside the company, who I made a point of contacting at least once a quarter. I'm aware that it was not just the connections I made that contributed to my successful career; rather, it was developing and nourishing those relationships year after year and finding ways to add value to them that made all the difference.

Shortly after I joined PepsiCo, I was approached by the American Management Association (AMA) to join their Finance Council. It was made up of financial and accounting executives from large corporations who met on a quarterly basis to discuss current professional developments, with an eye towards evaluating whether they were worthy of a new AMA course or program. I accepted the invitation because I knew this was a golden opportunity. On this Council, I met the CFO of Hershey Foods and the head of JP Morgan's London Office. They were the first members of my network, and it was the beginning of broadening my horizons.

For example, the contact from JP Morgan had many connections from his time stationed in London. He came to New York a lot, and we would have dinner together. He knew what was going on internationally and helped me to understand international banking business. In return, I gave him insight into what PepsiCo was looking for, which helped him to develop a better sales pitch. When you have strong relationships, you create a back door to talk about important developments, trends, and opportunities before they get hot and covered by the media. As JP Morgan had an account manager in New York who was entirely dedicated to handling Pepsi's needs, we didn't do any direct business. Our relationship went beyond that. We helped each other learn ways to become more effective in our roles. The benefits of these external relationships are tremendous. Look for opportunities to join councils or other organizations. You don't get paid, but you'll meet important people and get to talk about hot topics.

To enhance my personal development, I also asked my boss, Karl Vonder Heyden, if he could arrange for me to sit in on some regular corporate/business unit meetings, such as the monthly business review presentation of the annual operating plan and strategic plan. Not only was this a major opportunity to learn about the businesses, but it also raised my visibility level with corporate and division management. Karl had a passion for developing people, so he was more than happy to help me.

In executing Step Six, I would always look for ways to add value. The Annual Shareholders Meeting is a major event where shareholders and other interested parties can question management. To assist the CEO and Chairman, I developed a book of possible questions on "hot-button" issues and prepared answers that they could use in response. For example, we had a sculpture garden at the corporate office, and every year one of the shareholders would ask why we were wasting their money on sculptures. So I took a proactive approach and had the sculptures appraised before every Shareholder Meeting. That way, when someone asked the question, the Chairman could simply share the appraisal report to prove that the sculptures increased in value every year.

Building Relationships with Peers in Other Functions and Operating Units

To help position yourself for higher level positions, Step Six can provide you with a greater understanding of the business and its many key functions. This is true of every functional discipline; there is a commonality of interest throughout the company in forging close relationships. For example, it is the responsibility of the food scientists in the R & D department to develop new products, but they need help to know the financial impact and understand the economics. In turn, the financial people and the marketing team can help the R & D department to determine cost, pricing, and the marketing plan. It's important that you be constantly on the lookout for opportunities to collaborate and provide your expertise.

Likewise, improved communication between corporate financial professionals and their operating unit counterparts can improve decision-making and interpretation of information in financial reporting. Another benefit of working closely together is developing an appropriate comfort level in considering possible promotions and personnel moves. The fundamental point is this: having an in-depth knowledge of the business, as well as establishing relationships across the business, are key attributes that must be demonstrated if you want to progress into business leadership positions.

Most businesses are organized in silos or functional areas—tax people, legal people, accounting, etc. There's not a lot of overlap between these groups. They are located in separate parts of the building, and they stay within their groups. A common perception is that the corporate people have a higher status and the operating units are looked down upon. This is not correct. Every functional unit of the business is vital to the success of the whole. An accountant needs to understand marketing and build relationships with his or her colleagues in the marketing department. At the same time, a marketer has to understand how R & D works.

And when there are problems, you need to communicate with people from different departments. You should stay close to the operating people and get to know them. At Taco Bell, I had a rule that every accounting person had to work in one of our restaurants for one day every quarter. Even the Vice President making $200,000 a year had to spend half a day working at a Taco Bell. The only problem was that the accounting people couldn't do much other than give out drinks at the counter. Yet it still helped them understand what happens at the front line.

And when I worked at Frito-Lay, everyone on the team had to ride on a delivery route every few months. I couldn't do much to help out the driver, but I learned a lot. Riding on the truck, you'd see everything.

I'd ask the driver what products were moving the fastest. I saw the competitor's products on the shelves. The big advantage for Frito-Lay is that we had our own delivery system. We had 10,000 trucks on the road every day. Most food companies deliver to big warehouses, and the people in the individual stores put it on the shelves. But our delivery system brings the products directly to the stores and shelves them, so we can sort of control the shelf. Riding on the trucks really gave me a sense of how that strategy of control, of having our own sales force and controlling the shelves, was a key competitive advantage. As a result, we owned the salty snack category. Nobody was close to Frito-Lay when it came to potato chips, pretzels, and corn chips.

Some people didn't get the concept. They couldn't understand why it was important to be close to the field where the money was being made. They would say, "I went to Harvard, and now you're asking me to ride on a truck with a guy who didn't even finish high school?"

They didn't understand that the real world is in the supermarket and not in the corporate office. They all wanted to get into the boardroom and give speeches and make presentations. But it's more important to be hungry and street smart in order to make a meaningful contribution. It's about being unafraid to get into the field and see where the business really takes place, because the front lines are where the money is made.

The financial guys merely keep score. The core business is done in the streets and in the plants by lots of people, whether they're people working the line part-time at Taco Bell or delivering your products by truck. Those are the people who you need to lead, influence, and listen to.

I'd say to my teams, "The corporate world is like a bubble. Everyone around you is like you. That's not a good representation of the world or your company. In our case, the whole deal is selling chips. You must know what the customers are saying and what the competition is doing. The top of the pyramid is the CEO, but the people who are most important are those closest to the customers. In the end, what matters is selling something, and we sell successfully by staying close to the customers. We need to do everything we can do to support the sales team. It's a mistake to think that you don't need to know what is going on in the stores."

Building Relationships Outside Your Company

You have to build a treasure chest of contacts. That creates value because you have access to information that other people want. Due to PepsiCo's large presence in Latin America, I wanted to establish a relationship with a knowledgeable financial adviser in that region, and my network recommended Violy McCausland, a leading banker with JP Morgan.

In Latin America, businesses are run by families. Having the right connections and introductions is very important. Violy knew most of the affluent families that were involved in the large food and beverage companies. We built a relationship over the years, and when she left JP Morgan to start her own advisory firm, she asked me to join her Board of Advisors. The other Board members included former secretaries of finance in several key countries and a Mexican industrialist involved in the food business. Violy and I became good friends, and she became a member of my inner circle. She was instrumental in helping PepsiCo buy Gamesa, the large Mexican food company, because of her knowledge of the company's family dynamics.

In the U.S., it's mostly price that determines whether you'll close a deal, because that's in the best interests of the investors. But in other countries, relationships really matter more than the price. If you're doing business internationally, you need people with connections in every country. You need to have someone who has insight into and information about the culture and who understands the family relationships.

On the investment banking side, an area where I didn't have much experience, I established several important relationships. My brother-in-law, a partner at Goldman Sachs, introduced me to a senior banking partner and the vice Chairman of Goldman Sachs International, a former State Department official, who provided exceptional insights into foreign affairs and had many contacts in countries important to PepsiCo.

A network can give you tremendous insight. My contacts were extremely valuable when I needed help, yet I always made sure that once a relationship was established, it became a two-way street. I would also provide them with the information they needed. Obviously, you have to be careful not to give away any confidential information.

When you build and nurture a network of contacts, they can really help you with crucial information when you most need it.

Relationships Are a Two-Way Street

Communication must be regular and two-way. You must continually look for experiences and insights that are relevant for your network partner. You can't always call them asking them for something. You have to look for opportunities that will benefit them. Otherwise, the other person gets tired of you. You have to always ask yourself, "How can I help my key contacts?"

As I mentioned before, PepsiCo was the first company who took the Japanese subsidiary of an American company public on the Tokyo Stock Exchange. This was a big deal in finance. It had never been done before, and everyone wanted to know about it.

There were a number of Fortune 500 companies who were operating in Japan, but I only casually knew the CFOs of those companies. If you don't have a relationship with them, they won't take your calls. I needed to develop a relationship with them to expand my network of helpful contacts, so I put together a detailed package about the KFC issues and sent it to them. It was not proprietary information, and by doing this, I saved them hundreds of hours of research. In the white paper, I went through the process of how to list an American company on the Tokyo Stock Exchange, the advantages, the disadvantages, what I would do differently, etc. The CFOs appreciated it greatly, and it became such a valuable document that I still get calls about it to this day.

Another example of how I used valuable information to develop my network was when PepsiCo introduced Share Power. Stock options used to be offered only to very senior corporate executives. I was a member of the team that researched the possibility of giving all employees the right to buy stock options. We put together a white paper about it that included the legal and financial issues. I went through my list to determine which relationships I wanted to strengthen, and I sent them the white paper with a note that said, "I'm sure you've heard about PepsiCo's Share Power, and questions may be raised about stock options in your own company as well. You might be interested in learning more about the questions and the issues we dealt with."

The responses I received were very positive. Some of my contacts would ask me, "Why are you doing this?" And I'd tell them, "I respect you and I'd like to open up a dialogue with you, without sharing any confidential information, of course."

By continuously looking for ways to add value to other people, you build strong relationships that you can fall back on when needed. For a network to be effective and useful, it must be a two-way street in providing information and introductions. The key is to create a two-way communication that results in a win/win situation for all parties. Start looking for ways you can contribute to the success of others.

Creating Your Network

In putting Step Six into action, you may wonder, "Where do I start? How do I create my network?"

Establishing a network is not difficult, but you have to make it a priority. Here are five great ways to put Step Six into action by connecting with the right people:

1) Professional advisors like lawyers, consultants, auditors, and accountants often have industry specializations and may be able to provide introductions to executives of other companies in your industry. Tell them what you're trying to do and ask them to help you by making introductions.

Arthur Andersen & Company, the major accounting firm, did consulting work for PepsiCo. The consultant folks introduced me to senior partners in the audit and tax practice. By meeting regularly with these partners, I gained an additional perspective on SEC and tax matters and gained access to the partners in their foreign offices, who were closely tied in with local governments and successful business leaders, particularly in lesser-developed countries.

2) Former employees who have joined other companies are a good source. They are probably in similar jobs in their new companies. Ask them to introduce you to your counterpart in their organization. Even if I didn't know the person who left PepsiCo, I made it a practice to email them after a couple of weeks. I'd congratulate them on their new job and ask if they would be willing to introduce me to the person in my role at their new company.

3) Join professional organizations and trade associations. When you go to annual meetings and conventions, you'll naturally meet a lot of people who have similar interests. Make sure to bring and collect business cards, and, most importantly, to build relationships while you're there.

4) The CEO of your company may be on the board of another company. Every time my CEO joined a new board, I would reach out to the treasurer of that company. The CEO of PepsiCo was on the board of Chase, so the CFO of Chase and I would keep each other informed before the board meetings. In almost every case, my counterpart was happy to have open communication. And it always worked two ways. If certain issues came up on their board, he would give me a heads-up, and vice versa.

5) Your alumni office is a valuable resource. I would contact the alumni office of the Simon Business School and tell them I wanted to know everyone who worked for consumer products companies, especially any CFO, treasurer, and controller. I would email them and say, "We're both alumni of the Simon Business School, and I'd like to connect with you. I'm building my network, and I think we can be of value to each other." If the person wasn't the CFO, I'd ask him or her for an introduction. In nine out of the ten cases, it wasn't a problem, and they would send my bio to their CFO. Next thing you know, I'm on the phone with the CFO of another major company. Of course, if they were alumni from my class, it was even easier to reconnect.

Don't underestimate the power of your alumni network. When PepsiCo was looking to get into India, we ran into a lot of regulations affecting foreign companies. I called the alumni office and asked if there were any alumni working in India. They sent me the names, and I emailed Raj S., who was living in Punjab, an agricultural region in India. I didn't know him personally, as he had graduated ten years after me.

I wrote, "You're living in Punjab, and interestingly enough, Pepsi is looking to get into India. As you live there, can you tell me what we can expect? What kind of challenges will we face?"

Raj emailed me back a five-page paper about doing business in India and mentioned, "By the way, my brother is the minister of agriculture." When I shared this with my colleague, he said, "He's the decision maker we've been trying to contact for months without success." So I asked Raj, "Would it be at all possible to make an introduction so my colleague can meet with your brother when he's in India in three weeks?" His response? Give me the dates and I'll get it done. That's the power of having alumni connections.

In India, they wouldn't allow us to name the product Pepsi Cola because they wanted an Indian name. Once again, I went to my network in India to find out how to overcome the challenge and discovered that there was a way around it.

The people in your network are your tentacles into the outside world. They can provide you with the knowledge that gives you power. It allows you to find out what people are talking about in other places, not just in your own company. My connection at Goldman Sachs introduced me to a restaurant analyst. At the time, I wanted to become the internal restaurant expert in PepsiCo. We had lunch together, and I asked her if she would be willing to add me to the mailing lists of clients that received their quarterly reports. The restaurant analyst agreed, and it turned out to be a valuable source to know what was going on competitively. If there was an article in the newspaper about a new development at Chipotle, I'd call her to ask if there was more to the story. She was a full-time analyst and knew what was going on in the industry.

Having relationships with successful business people outside your own company will make an important contribution to your personal and career development. Finding peers in similar jobs in other companies can provide for mutually beneficial conversations on subjects of common interest. Furthermore, they can provide introductions to professionals in similar functions at other companies. Last but not least, they can share leads on openings in other corporations.

STEP #6. TAKEAWAYS!

Developing business relationships inside and outside of your company can be a major asset in accelerating your career. You can learn from peers, who will provide you with insights and sources of information about areas where you do not have experience or expertise. By reaching out to alumni of your college and to former associates who have joined other companies, you can identify contacts and gain introductions that will build your network.

Here are the specific steps you can take to put Step Six into action.

Takeaway No. 1: Join associations and groups related to your area of expertise. There are numerous trade groups and councils that you can join to meet your peers in other companies and industries. That is what I did, and it enabled me to build an important network that helped propel my climb through the corporate ranks.

Takeaway No. 2: Cultivate contacts with a strategic focus in mind. When you have strong relationships, you can create a back door to talk about important developments, trends, and opportunities before they get hot and covered by the media. Through this exchange of information, I was able to establish mutually beneficial arrangements, whereby my contacts and I could exchange information of strategic importance to our respective companies.

Takeaway No. 3: Ask to join key meetings. I asked if I could attend corporate/business unit meetings, such as the monthly presentation of PepsiCo's annual operating plan and strategic plan. Not only was this a major opportunity to learn about the businesses, but it also raised my visibility level with corporate and division management.

Takeaway No. 4: Always look for ways to add value by taking proactive actions to raise your visibility. To assist the CEO and Chairman of PepsiCo, I developed a list of possible questions and prepared answers on "hot-button" issues that could arise at the Annual Shareholders Meeting. This helped the CEO with his presentation and greatly raised my visibility with him.

Takeaway No. 5: Know the business and its many key functions, especially the key functions of units other than your own. Understanding your business and its many key functions is essential. For example, in addition to the financial side, you need to become familiar with R & D and marketing in order look for opportunities to collaborate and provide your expertise. You can't do that if you don't know your business inside and out. Having in-depth knowledge of your business and establishing relationships across the business are key attributes that must be demonstrated in order for you to progress into leadership positions.

Takeaway No. 6: Stay close to the operating people. I always stayed close to the operating people and got to know them. Otherwise, you lose touch with the fundamentals of your business. At Taco Bell, I had a rule that every accounting person had to work in one of our restaurants for one day every quarter. Even the Vice President making $200,000 a year had to spend half a day working at a Taco Bell. The real world is on the front lines and not in the corporate office. When you lose sight of the front lines, you're more likely to make decisions that will negatively affect the business.

Takeaway No. 7: The corporate world is a bubble that needs to be punctured. The corporate world is like a bubble—it doesn't represent the world or your company. The top of the pyramid is the CEO, but the people who are most important are those closest to the customers. You must know what the customers are saying and what the competition is doing. It's a big mistake to think that you don't need to know what's happening on the ground level.

Takeaway No. 8: When doing international business, the right connections and introductions are very important. Understanding the business culture of a foreign country is imperative when conducting international transactions. Without the understanding I gained of Mexican business culture through one of my contacts, the Gamesa deal would not have happened.

Takeaway No. 9: Relationships should be a two-way street. My contacts were extremely valuable when I needed help, yet I always made sure that once a relationship was established I provided my network with quality information that would help them. This kind of exchange must be a two-way street in order to work.

Takeaway No. 10: Use valuable information to develop your network. I was a member of the team that researched the possibility of giving all employees the right to buy stock options. I shared the white paper I developed on this topic with my key contacts outside the company. By doing so, I was able to open up a meaningful dialogue with them without sharing any confidential information.

The Next Step!

Part of building relationships is finding the right person who can help guide your career in a personalized, one-on-one manner. Without that key relationship, I never would have risen as high as I did in the corporate ranks. Which leads us to Step Seven—finding and making the most of a mentor.

Chapter Eight

Step #7. Learning from the Masters by Finding a Mentor

Finding the right mentor was a key factor in my career success, and it can be the same in your career development and entry into higher management. I was fortunate to have amazing bosses at PepsiCo, each considered a titan in his field. They taught me every aspect of the business. In addition, as a junior executive, you need to understand the etiquette, politics, and unwritten rules of your company's culture if you want to progress up the ranks. A mentor can help you do that.

My first boss was Karl Vonder Heyden, a German accountant and financial manager, who taught me the difference between being an accountant and being a financial manager in an operating environment. While the preparation of financial statements is the final product of the accountant, the financial manager or controller seeks to analyze and interpret the results, address the "so what?" questions and implications, and identify areas of risk.

Karl was more than just my boss—he was a terrific mentor. The dictionary defines a mentor as an experienced and trusted advisor, and that is what Karl was. Every quarter, we visited the operating divisions together to meet with the division CFO, the controller, and representatives of our outside auditors to review the results, the financial position of the division, and any risks or exposures. Karl was very thorough in his questioning and took diligent notes.

Karl's disciplined approach and insightful questions provided the platform that enabled me to grow outside the narrow "bean counter" role.

Karl always wanted to meet and interact with new members of the accounting and financial staffs and was always on the lookout for bright, young professionals in the accounting firms. This focus on the yearly identification of talent and the monitoring of their development became a core part of my regimen and belief system. In order to broaden my operating perspective, Karl arranged for me to attend Strategic Plan and Annual Operating Plan Reviews.

Karl's wise use of financial information to influence business decision-making led to his quick rise through the ranks. He became CFO of Pepsi Cola Company and Vice Chairman of the PepsiCo Board of Directors. He then left PepsiCo to become CFO of Heinz and then CEO of RJR-Nabisco.

Learning the Unwritten Rules

I also had the privilege of working for PepsiCo founder and former CEO Don Kendall in the latter years of his career. He was very well respected. When he said something at a meeting, everybody would listen very carefully. Although Don had given up operating responsibilities, he still had his own office and regularly counseled Pepsi managers, franchisee bottlers, and world leaders who had come to rely on Don's judgment and advice.

My office was eight doors down the hall from Don's, and when his door was open and he wasn't busy, I'd take the opportunity to speak with him. He invited me to accompany him on market tours, and he taught me the importance of going beyond the financials and seeing the businesses up close. Of course, the market tours were carefully orchestrated. Every factory and store puts its best foot forward when expecting a visit from the top brass. That's why Don advised me to always arrange for my own car. That way, I could break away from the choreographed tour and see the real market.

When I did that, I could talk to the store owners about what was going on in the market and what the competition was doing. I'd look at how much space we had versus how much space Coke had. I would get insights into what the stores needed or wanted from corporate.

This was the era of returnable bottles. By breaking away from the choreographed tour and seeing the real market, I found out that a lot of returnable bottles were piling up at stores because we weren't picking them up on a timely basis. As a result, there was a lot of breakage, and that meant more money spent on bottles. We knew we had to do a better job of picking up the bottles. I would have missed this entirely if I had stuck to the choreographed tour.

Don had a wide network of contacts all over the world that went far beyond titled executives; they provided him independent insights and perspectives. He had keen insight into geopolitical matters, which provided me with important input in managing foreign exchange and international risk exposures.

Every company has its own culture. As a junior executive, you need to understand the etiquette, politics, and unwritten rules if you want to progress up the ranks. As my mentor, Don explained the unwritten rules and etiquette for PepsiCo junior executives. He taught me how to behave in meetings. He'd tell me, "Len, as a junior executive, you have to understand that you can't just grab the microphone and speak up at a meeting with senior executives, regardless of how valuable the point is that you want to make. People don't appreciate that. If you have a good idea or feedback, why don't you write a note with your thoughts and send it to the person? They will appreciate it."

He gave me practical ideas that I used effectively. In the beginning, I was just an observer, sitting to the side. But when there was a coffee break, I made it a point to talk to the senior guys and make a contribution privately. After the meeting, I'd go up to someone and say, "You made a very good comment about XYZ. I was thinking about it, and based on the numbers I've seen it's a very valid point, because. . . ." I was always looking for a way to add value to the company, rather than just impressing people or making a name for myself. It worked well, because over time people began to call me and seek my counsel before the meetings.

Management by "Wandering About"

Don showed me many times that the little things matter and make a big difference. Before he visited a plant, he assembled a book with pictures of every employee and notes about them. He would memorize information about each and every person. Don would go in and say, "Hi Caroline, how's your son? Did he get into West Point?" Or he would say, "Hello Simon. What's going on your life? Is there anything getting in the way of you doing a great job?"

The employees were blown away that the president of the company knew something about them and cared about what was going on in their lives. They might be earning just the minimum wage, yet the president of the company was interested in them. Don always remembered and connected with the employees—and that meant a lot.

It was Don's exemplary leadership that inspired me to start "management by wandering about." The top executives have their own floor, where a chef is making them breakfast, lunch, and dinner. They have the tendency to stay in their ivory tower. Don taught me that a leader has to be visible. You have to put yourself out there on a regular basis. You can't lead from a corporate suite. People need to know who you are. When you don't leave the executive floor, you talk to the same people every day, and you lose sight of what's really going on in the company.

Every couple of days, I would visit the people working for me. That's how I got to know them. John Tirino was my compass. He was a long-time employee who had worked at PepsiCo for more than thirty years. When we did our cafeteria day together, we would walk from table to table, and he would say, "Len, you should hear what Betty is working on." We would sit down, and Betty would tell me her story. By mingling, I learned what was going on. I got to know them, and they became familiar with me.

After each cafeteria day, I made a list of people I had met. Johnnie would find out their birthdays, and he would send a card on my behalf. It's a little thing, but the employees valued it greatly. The executive has to get out of his or her bubble.

"Management by wandering about" also enabled me to find smart people. As a good leader, you want to find the talent in your company. By establishing your network internally, you'll be able to spot the stars who have potential. Or whenever I had a new idea, I would ask John what he thought about it. He'd say, "It's a good idea, but somebody tried it ten years ago. It didn't work because of XYZ." And I knew not to pursue it.

There are John Tirinos in every company. You just have to find them. They may not be a big name in the company or have a big title, but they're extremely valuable as conduits between the employees and the executive team. And as "company historians" who've been around for a while, they can alert you about lessons learned in the past that will prevent you from making mistakes.

No discussion of leadership at PepsiCo and its impact on my development would be complete without mentioning the important lessons I took away from Wayne Calloway and Michael Jordan. While both grew up on the financial side of the house, they were exceptional business leaders and warm human beings.

Wayne was particularly influential in counseling me on my career development and orchestrating my move to Frito-Lay. Michael Jordan, the senior VP at headquarters, is probably the brightest person I have ever encountered. Not only does he have a degree in nuclear engineering, but he is also a brilliant strategic thinker. We were reunited at Frito-Lay, where we teamed up to turnaround and re-energize that business. Michael's mind was so sharp and quick that I often had to translate his ideas for the senior staff. No one would challenge him.

Michael and I became close colleagues because he felt that I was less political and would give him frank opinions. One of the reasons he appreciated me was because he wanted a different viewpoint—someone he could bounce his ideas off of—and I served in that role. He told people that I was his "consigliere."

Andy Pearson, PepsiCo's former President, was a brilliant strategist. His ability to penetrate an issue and to always identify the soft spot in your presentation taught me to be ultra-analytical and to address potential alternative scenarios and explanations. This rigor became a part of my DNA.

Achieving Fast-Track Success without "Pissing Off" Your Boss

Finding a mentor can be an important element in your career development and entry into higher management. A mentor can help you become someone who has a greater impact on the company.

Many ask, "Isn't my boss my mentor?" Sometimes this can be the case, as it was for me. But in general, it's better not to consider your boss as your mentor. Your boss may see you as competition for her job and become afraid that you'll get promoted and jump over her. Your success in following the Eight Step Program may start to overshadow your boss. Besides, she has many people working for her and may not be able to dedicate the needed time that makes a mentoring relationship effective.

To avoid possible negative consequences from this, I have found it useful to do the following:

- Treat your boss with respect. Keep him or her informed about your activities, particularly those outside of his or her area.

- When your networking contacts provide you with insights or a discovery that might be of interest to your boss, be sure to share it. Offer to connect your boss with his counterpart at a company in your network.

- Most companies have some sort of performance appraisal and an annual salary increase process. At that time of year, prepare a summary of your accomplishments and send it to your boss. This will help him to prepare the evaluation, and, since some of your activities may have occurred months ago, ensures that they will not be forgotten and are properly included in your review.

It should be recognized that your success may put you in competition with your boss for promotional opportunities. However, in most companies, this is not a zero sum game. Your success or promotion does not mean your boss has failed or lacks other career growth opportunities within the company. And, as previously mentioned, in many companies the ability to develop future leaders is considered a major plus.

Nevertheless, it's important to have some direct connection with your boss's boss. An easy, nonthreatening way is to forward short notes with business insights or information nuggets derived from your networking activities that say, "FYI, thought you might find this of interest." Showing this type of initiative, in and of itself, adds value to the company but may also lead to further conversations that can benefit you directly.

Finding a Mentor

Your mentor is like a guide through the jungle. Together, you develop an action plan to get you where you want to go. But what makes an effective mentoring relationship?

Find someone with a similar background who has made it up to the higher tier. You need someone who understands what it takes to get to the higher ranks. Sometimes it can be a CFO or a similar high-ranking executive from another company—someone inside the company who understands its dynamics. Everyone would like to be mentored by the CEO, but that's not feasible. Or it can be someone no longer working for your company. I chose a retired Pepsi founder who knew more about PepsiCo than anyone else.

What are the qualities of a mentor? A mentor is somebody who is willing to help, has the time, and is interested in you. If he or she is too busy to spend the time with you, it won't work. A casual mentor is not a good mentor. You need somebody with whom you have a great deal of chemistry, as there needs to be a high level of likeability. A mentorship is an interactive relationship. You can't mentor someone from a distance or if you don't connect.

Your mentor should help you position yourself as a future member of the senior management team. You want others to view you as a person with broad management skills and as a strategic thinker, someone who has more to offer than just being a bean counter. While your boss is important to your development and can help you excel in your silo, your mentor helps you break out of your silo. But in order to do that, you have to be very open to receiving feedback and willing to accept constructive criticism. The role of the mentor is to provide you with candid advice, help guide you through the political maze, and move you into the senior ranks.

But how do you find a mentor? Obviously, there's a lot of competition in finding one. You have to look beyond the obvious. I'm often asked, "How can I establish that kind of personal relationship with a busy senior executive?" If you follow the guidance provided in Chapter Three, you will undoubtedly meet potential mentor candidates. You'll have to sell yourself to the mentor to convince them that they should spend time with you, because he or she probably gets many requests. You'll have to show them that you are a world-class accountant and strategic thinker who can help build a good organization.

I've found the corporate fitness center to be a great spot to meet executives. While waiting for a piece of equipment, it may be easy to strike up a conversation. A wonderful, often overlooked source of mentors is the company's retired executives. They often have the time, and, with a likely significant equity stake, an incentive in helping develop the next generation of leaders.

Mentoring is particularly important in professions or industries where there have been barriers preventing movement into executive management—for example, the barriers facing women on Wall Street. The organization Elevation (formerly 85 Broads) was formed by successful female executives in the financial services area to help younger women move up in the ranks. Their frequent networking events and ladyship training sessions provide an excellent boost to women in the financial services area. To address the lack of black accountants in senior positions in CPA firms and corporations, the National Association of Black Accountants was created.

In recognition of the limited number of woman in technology leadership positions, several of the major Silicon Valley companies have joined together in a program to attract, coach, and mentor women in technology and computer science engineering. As a fast-tracker, you should investigate these groups to expand your network outside your company and to possibly find a mentor.

Developing an Effective Mentoring Relationship

From my experience, mentoring relationships tend to take two forms. The first is the "casual advisor" mentorship, where the mentor tells "war stories" about his career progression, and then suggests that the mentee contact him whenever he or she has a specific question or issue to discuss. In my experience, the informality of this type of mentorship rarely produces significant results.

In the more structured mentorship, the mentor and mentee develop a plan that sets forth objectives, specific plans, and timetables to accomplish; they then meet on a regular basis to review progress or to "correct course." This second type of mentorship is considerably more effective because rapport is formed, and the resulting serious discussion will be more likely to get you from where you are to where you want to be.

Before meeting with your mentor, you should be prepared to address the following questions. What is the "book" on you? How do others perceive your strengths and developmental needs? What is your next position target, and what is holding you back from achieving it? What skills are you lacking? Leadership skills? Other skills? What positions fit your personality?

Together with your mentor, you will develop a plan to address these issues. To illustrate this, I'll share one such plan from my own experience. The objective was to be more impactful at business strategy sessions. The plan included the following elements, which my mentor and I discussed during a two-hour session.

- Preparing for the meeting
- Meeting protocols (as a junior executive, there were certain protocols that I had to follow)
- Cues on the proper time to make a point
- Post-meeting follow-up

By following this process, I was able to understand the group dynamics and make a positive contribution. In addition, the post-meeting conversations and follow-up proved to be a critical element in properly raising my profile as a strategic thinker.

Benefiting from Role Models

In addition to having a mentor, you can also find and emulate a role model. In every business, there are highly successful leaders who have great qualities and skills worth emulating. You won't have a formal relationship with them, but you can informally observe and identify what they're doing that makes them successful. Michael Jordan and Wayne Calloway were my role models. I watched them carefully, made notes about how they conducted themselves and interacted with others, and made sure to follow their examples whenever I could. You can do the same.

STEP #7. TAKEAWAYS!

Step Seven—finding a mentor and developing an effective mentoring relationship—can be crucial in securing a pathway into senior management. In addition, identifying role models in your company and learning from their habits and behaviors can provide insight into what it takes to rise into the highest senior management ranks.

Here are specific ways to put Step Seven into action:

Takeaway No. 1: A mentor can explain the unwritten rules and etiquette of your corporate culture, as well as teach you key leadership skills. Every company has its own culture. As a junior executive, you need to understand the etiquette, politics, and unwritten rules if you want to progress up the ranks. At the same time, a mentor will teach you key leadership skills, such as "management by wandering about," which I learned from Don Kendall.

Takeaway No. 2: In general, it's better not to consider your boss as your mentor. Your boss may see you as competition for her job, and become afraid that you'll get promoted and jump over her. Besides, she has many people working for her and may not be able to dedicate the necessary time that makes a mentorship relationship effective.

Takeaway No. 3: A mentor can be someone from outside or no longer working for your company. Your mentor can be a high-ranking executive from another company—someone inside the company who understands its dynamics. Everyone would like to be mentored by the CEO, but that's not feasible. I chose a retired Pepsi founder. He knew more about PepsiCo than anyone else.

Takeaway No. 4: A casual mentorship relationship doesn't work. Your mentor must have the time, be interested in you, and have chemistry with you. It doesn't work if it's a casual relationship. If he or she is too busy to spend the time with you, it won't work. A mentorship is an interactive relationship. You can't mentor someone from a distance or if you don't connect.

Takeaway No. 5: Your boss helps you excel in your silo, but your mentor helps you break out of your silo. Your boss is key in helping you succeed in your current duties, but it is your mentor who will help you break out of your silo and fast-track your corporate career.

Takeaway No. 6: In a mentoring relationship, you must be open to receiving constructive criticism. The role of the mentor is to provide you with candid advice, help guide you through the political maze, and move you into the senior ranks. To succeed at this, you must be willing to accept constructive criticism.

Takeaway No. 7: Seek out organizations that can help mentor you. There are many professional organizations that can possibly provide you with a mentor.

Takeaway No. 8: Establish a structured mentorship. You and your mentor should develop a plan that sets forth objectives, specific plans, and timetables to accomplish. You should then meet on a regular basis to review progress or to "correct course." Having a plan will be more likely to get you where you want to be.

Takeaway No. 9: You can also emulate role models. In addition to a mentor, you can also find and emulate role models. In every business, there are highly successful leaders who have great qualities and skills worth emulating. You should observe, identify, and emulate those qualities and approaches that are making them successful.

The Next Step!

Just as you became a leader with the help of your mentor, you too can guide others to become leaders. In this way, you guarantee the success of the company down the line. The eighth and final step is about leaving a legacy behind by passing on your wisdom and expertise to those who will follow in your footsteps.

Chapter Nine

Step #8. Attract and Develop Future Leaders

Developing future leaders not only benefits the company but will help you accelerate your ascent up the corporate ladder. Early in my career, I volunteered to accompany our recruiters on their campus visits to identify talent, and in my networking, I was always on the lookout for people who would be a good fit at PepsiCo. The ability to attract, develop, and retain exceptional talent is an important factor in being considered for senior leadership promotions.

In my role as Treasurer at PepsiCo, it was an exciting time to expand the company while also mentoring the next generation leaders. To use a sports team analogy, an effective leader is measured by his ability to recruit and develop high talent players and direct them in superior execution. Your job is to get things done. Being viewed as an effective coach with outstanding leadership skills is essential if you want to become a fast-tracker.

In explaining Step Eight to you, I first have to make a detour and tell you about the event that changed my life.

A Call to 911

During an extremely busy week in 1992, a few days before Christmas, I had an appointment to make a presentation at a rating agency in downtown Manhattan. I decided to walk instead of taking a taxi. I was early for my appointment, so I stopped by my favorite coffee shop on Wall Street. Little did I know that my world would be turned completely upside down in just a few seconds.

I had had a headache in the morning and was feeling a little under the weather, but didn't think it was a big deal. Drinking my cup of coffee, I was beginning to feel worse and worse. But I was down there with a job to do, and I brushed it aside. And then I started feeling a little dizzy. I looked at my watch and saw I had twenty minutes before I was supposed to be at the rating agency. I got up from the chair and immediately collapsed to the floor. There was a lot of commotion around me, and people came running over.

"Call 911! Someone call 911!"

Lying there on the floor, all I was thinking was that I had to get myself together, get up, and go to my damned meeting. I was a fairly young guy, only in my forties. I was a runner and in pretty good shape. I thought perhaps I was just dehydrated or something. I knew I had to get up and get back to work. In retrospect, this was insane.

People in the coffee shop were loosening my tie and taking my jacket off, telling me I wasn't going anywhere, but I was in denial—total denial. I didn't believe it was serious.

I was rushed to St. Mary's Hospital in an ambulance. Even at the hospital, I was trying to talk my way out of it. I told the people in the emergency room that I wasn't really that bad off.

"I shouldn't be here. Just get me a cab, so I can go. I've got a meeting to go to."

Then the docs told me, "You're in the middle of having a stroke."

I was in critical condition and lost consciousness. The doctors didn't know whether I would make it. A priest came to see me. I'm Jewish, but I didn't care.

I'd take any help I could get. PepsiCo immediately sent a car to pick up my wife and children. When I regained consciousness, I was paralyzed. Although I was still alive, nothing was the same anymore.

I was still in denial. I didn't believe it could happen to me. I knew I couldn't move, but I kept rationalizing that I had some other kind of issue, even though I had no control over the left side of my body. My arm and leg were limp. I couldn't stand, I couldn't move anything.

The doctors said they had to keep me in the hospital for a period of time until I stabilized. They said I had a blockage in blood flow to the brain, and a lot of serious things could happen. If I stabilized, I then faced another two months in rehab to learn to walk again.

When the reality started to sink in, I became a bit depressed. I didn't know if I was ever going to return to work or if I was going to be in some sort of handicapped state for a long period of time. My son and daughter were very worried about me, which made me more nervous.

All my life, I had planned for every contingency, but I hadn't planned for this. You don't plan on dying when you've got young kids, you're not that old, and you've had good health throughout your life. The thoughts kept rushing through my mind: "I just hope I can get out of this. I hope I can get to a point where I'm still alive and still functioning."

I was in the rehab center for close to eight weeks, and I was a very bad patient. I always thought I could do more than I was able to do. That's what happens with overachievers. I thought I had to get better fast. They said, "You can't do this yet, you're in a wheelchair." But I'd say, "I'm going to do it." I'd put my mind to it. I had always been able to do what I wanted. But I couldn't, and I would fall down, and the physical therapists would say, "Hey, you can't do this stuff. You've got to listen to us. You need someone to help you do everything."

After about a month in rehab, I was invited by Don Kendall to a special event. Don had traveled to Russia many times and had become friends with President Mikhail Gorbachev and his wife. The Gorbachevs were in New York, and Don arranged a dinner for them at PepsiCo with a select group of people. I was thrilled to be invited.

The doctors at the rehab center felt it was premature for me to consider going. I protested, accelerating my exercise and strength training. This was a once-in-a-lifetime opportunity to meet the Gorbachevs, as well as a chance to show that I was still a player and able to contribute.

I finally convinced the doctors to let me go. This was my first time out of the hospital, and I was nervous that I would fall with my walker or spill food on my tuxedo.

President Gorbachev and his wife were so pleasant and understanding. Fortunately, everything went well. My ability to function in this setting was a huge morale and confidence booster.

The following week, I returned to PepsiCo on a part-time basis. It felt great to be back, and I experienced no difficulties in doing my work. I had a driver who took me into the office, and I had a very good staff. I had no inclination other than to stay at PepsiCo for the long haul. I was back talking to people overseas and connecting with my network, so I was pretty optimistic that everything was going to work out fine.

I was in the middle of reviewing the financial reports when Roger King, the head of human resources, walked into my office. He sat down and asked, "Len, do you have a minute? I need to talk to you."

I could tell that it was going to be a serious topic, but I never expected what he said next.

"We greatly appreciate the work you've done for PepsiCo for so many years, but we're concerned that your job has more pressure than you can handle."

I was somewhat in shock. "What are you saying, Roger? I may be handicapped, but I'm only in my forties. I still have the ability to lead, and I still have my intellect. It's only the left side of my body that's paralyzed. My mental capacity and speech are unaffected."

"I understand, Len. We just don't want to have it on our conscience if anything happens to you. You'll be taken care of. You'll receive full disability until you're sixty-five years old."

This was a very difficult time for me. I loved my job and felt too young to be sent home. But as one of my friends told me, "You can't be a member of a club that doesn't want you."

And he was right. As hurt as I was that they were putting me out to pasture, I started to realize that there were benefits to receiving the disability package. It would allow me to start a new career without financial concerns.

My Farewell Dinner

The restaurant was filling up quickly. After eighteen years at PepsiCo, I had many friends in the company. Dave, the owner of Valbella, my favorite Italian restaurant in Connecticut, had offered to personally cook my farewell dinner. Over the years, I had enjoyed many delicious meals at his restaurant. I would often bring mentees there for meetings. It was great to see everyone who attended the dinner, as they brought back so many stories and memories.

As soon as everyone had taken a seat, David Rader stood up to make a toast. I had met David right after I joined PepsiCo, when I visited Frito-Lay for the annual operating plan review in 1986. When I met him, he was a young man who explained to me the pricing structure at Frito-Lay, and I was impressed with his analysis and the new insights he had gained from recent market research.

"Thank you all for coming," David began. "It's an honor and a privilege to be here, especially because Len has been such a great mentor and has become a good friend. I well remember the day that I met Len, since it was the first time that I presented to the PepsiCo senior management group.

"Len walked up to me after the presentation, told me that he was impressed, and asked me to tell him more about my background. I told him that I had previously worked for the Chrysler Corporation as a financial analyst and had joined PepsiCo to enhance my career, but felt stuck. Len explained that developing talent in the financial group was one of his top priorities, and this brief conversation began a thirty-year business and personal relationship.

"Len explained that I had to broaden my horizons. I remember him telling me, 'David, you can't be just an analyst. You need to have a good grasp of international accounting and reporting.' Every time Len came to Dallas, we would have lunch or dinner together, and he taught me what I should do to fast-track my career.

"A few years later, Len became the CFO of Taco Bell, and he hired me as the VP of Planning. I worked closely with David Sagal, Taco Bell's controller, becoming educated on the basics of financial reporting and the development of financial systems. This was critical if I was to move into the CFO ranks one day—and it worked.

"When PepsiCo created a new division to handle the purchasing and distribution for all its restaurants, I was selected as its CFO, which was very exciting! Len and I stayed in touch over the years. When his short stint as CFO of Frito-Lay ended, he advocated for me as his replacement. At the time, the CEO selected another candidate, but when the position opened up a few years later, I was given my dream job."

"I am very grateful for the lessons Len taught me," David went on, "and that he could see my leadership abilities. He is the one who taught me the eight steps to fast-track my career. Once I gained broader experience, new doors of opportunity opened. If it weren't for him, I probably would still be an analyst to this day. He not only showed me the path; he took me under his wing and propelled me forward. Thank you so much, Len! You are an incredible man, and my life is better because our paths crossed."

His toast earned major applause. Then, I stood up.

"Thank you, David, for your beautiful words," I said. "I'm very proud of you, and it's great to see how you have developed into a leader. Michael is fortunate to have you as the CFO of Frito-Lay. I admire you, David, and I'm proud of you."

David was your typical mid-western kind of guy. He wasn't loud but knew how to deal with people in a soft-spoken way. He was very smart and very willing to learn. David went on to become the Gold Standard of CFOs at PepsiCo.

Next, Jay Kushner stood up. "I remember the day I met Len Schutzman like it was yesterday," he said. "I was engrossed in researching an esoteric section of the Internal Revenue Code when I looked up and saw Len walk into my cubicle. Although I knew that Len was my boss's boss, I had never formally met him. My heart skipped a beat. I wondered why he would come to see me. Nobody from the executive floor had ever come down to the tax department.

If they wanted something, they would summon my boss to the rarified air of the executive floor. I wasn't sure what to expect, but Len put me at ease quickly.

"He said, 'Hi Jay, I'm Len Schutzman. I saw your name copied on an email regarding some interesting tax planning ideas on sourcing arising from new IRS regulations. Since I'm interested in learning more, I wanted to take the opportunity to come and meet you and get educated about this.'

"I was surprised, to say the least. Len inquired about my background and then went on to explain how this new tax development might impact PepsiCo's strategic planning. While I knew that the research indicated that there could be a lower tax rate, I didn't realize that it could also impact the strategic planning and treasury management. Len suggested that we periodically get together to review progress on this project, and he invited me to sit in on the next staff meeting of the Treasury Group to brief them on this concept.

"This unexpected encounter with Len was the beginning of my relationship with him. Later, he explained to me the concept of 'management by walking about,' and why, as an executive, it was important to not get stuck on the executive floor but to penetrate the organization. This was one of the many valuable lessons he taught me about becoming a leader in the company.

"Over the next several months, I worked closely with Len and his team to identify tax-planning strategies that would enhance the bottom line and increase shareholder value, while he mentored me and prepared me for more senior positions. Len's interest in my development opened the door of my cubicle—suddenly I could see new career opportunities, and I was promoted to Director of International Tax Planning.

"Len's mentorship has been of tremendous value. He showed me the path to fast-track my career. As I learned more about the interaction between tax and treasury, I developed sufficient perspective to manage both functions, and this led to my current position of Senior Vice President of Global Taxation and Treasury at Viacom. Thank you, Len, for your friendship and for being the best mentor I could wish for."

"It was a pleasure working with you, Jay," I said, "and if I had the chance, I would hire you back any day. I knew that the quality of your thinking and your creativity would serve you well in life if you had the right mentorship."

John Tirino stood up. "I, too, am grateful that Len walked into my life. You see, I'm not a big shot. I don't have a fancy title or a college degree. I worked at Pepsi Cola concentrate accounting, and I was surprised to have Len drop by one day. He had been appointed assistant controller, and he was walking around to get to know people. I've worked for a lot of people during my many years with PepsiCo, but no one from upper management had ever come down to talk to me.

"Len and I became good friends. We would walk around the cafeteria together on a regular basis, and I can tell you it made a big difference for everyday people like me on the work floor. It was inspiring to know that someone cared about what we had to say. Len would ask for my feedback on his ideas and wanted to hear what we were working on. We missed you when you left, Len, but we'll never forget you."

It was touching to hear the stories of my protégées and to see firsthand that my Eight Step process had had such amazing results. Looking around the room, it was exciting to see how many people had come—and how many of them were running big companies. I saw John Cahill, the CEO of Kraft Foods, sitting next to Tom Davin, the CEO of Panda Restaurant Group, and Miguel Colado, the President of Dean Foods International.

In addition to corporate leadership positions, a few went on to apply their talents in non-profit organizations. Matt McKenna, one of my hires in the tax group, became CEO of Keep America Beautiful. Shauna King, who was a young financial and marketing analyst at Frito-Lay, became the CFO of Yale University. Charlie Feld, my information and systems director at Frito-Lay, went on to start a consulting firm that he sold to EDS and created an information technology think tank, the Feld Organization.

My thoughts were interrupted by the sound of Larry Meyer's knife tinkling against glass, as he was getting ready to speak next.

"Even before I met Len," Larry began, "I knew that he was a man worth learning from. I was working as a financial analyst in the Pepsi Cola USA unit when I read the announcement of Len's promotion to CFO of Pepsi Bottling International. With my background in accounting and an MBA from Columbia Business School, I recognized that this could be a great opportunity for me to possibly secure a position in that division. However, knowing that Len had an incredible network of contacts in finance jobs around PepsiCo, I felt my chances were slim. Fortunately, I heard that one of the managers in the Pepsi USA division, Larry Bouts, had a job interview with Len, and I asked if he could present my qualifications and interest in a position in Pepsi Bottling International. Thanks to Larry's recommendation, I was invited for an interview for a managerial position in the planning group, and Len offered me the job.

"My first assignment was to benchmark the international bottling units against U.S. counterparts of comparable volume. I presented a twenty-five-page report with numbers and graphs, but Len asked me to distill the information into a PowerPoint presentation and only focus on the most important insights and implications. Len reviewed it, and I had to present my findings to my senior financial staff.

"After the presentation, Len sat down with me. He complimented me on the thoroughness of my work, and then said, 'Larry, you are a very bright young man, but you think and talk so fast that most people can't keep up with you. Your presentation style doesn't convey the depth of your thinking. When you jump from one idea to another, you lose your audience and don't have the desired impact. The difference between being a bright financial analyst and a senior manager is often in the presentation. Plus, if you want to be promoted, you have to be reflective. Ask yourself: Why should this person be interested in this? That way, you'll come across as a senior, not a junior guy.' He also emphasized the importance of thinking through, in advance, the key points to make on each slide and pulling it all together with a compelling conclusion and call-to-action.

"At first, I had a little bit of a hard time accepting his feedback. But I decided to put his suggestions into action, and, by slowing down a bit, I improved my presentations significantly. I noticed that the response to my presentations improved and that people grasped my message much more quickly. At the same time, people began to view me as a thoughtful financial manager rather than just a good analyst and numbers jockey. After six months, I was promoted to Regional Finance Director for Europe and Asia. Len gave me the opportunity to grow into the job and have a meaningful impact on business strategies. Thanks to his mentorship, my communication skills continued to improve, which was valuable, as I had to interact more frequently with senior division and corporate executives. Len's mentoring provided a clear roadmap into more senior jobs, first as CFO, and ultimately as the president of a global retail business. Thank you, Len. I appreciate the opportunity you've given me to fast-track my career."

I was very grateful for Larry's words. One of the most important keys to fast-tracking the corporate ladder is learning to write and communicate effectively, which the Larry's story proves. He was very smart and a fast thinker, but when he gave a presentation, he would tell you *everything* he knew; he wasn't focused. Larry had to learn that business people don't read more than five pages, and a PowerPoint presentation shouldn't be more than fifteen minutes long. Being focused in your communication skills is a vitally important skill to master.

"When I first met you, Larry," I said, "I was impressed with your passion for the soft drink business, but I was a little concerned about whether you could make the jump from an analyst position to a managerial job in a very important area. You have insightful business analytic skills and a drive for results. Under your leadership, an extremely difficult refranchising effort was successfully completed in six months, well ahead of the timeline we originally presented. Larry, it has been a pleasure working with you. To watch you flourish and thrive as you have would make any mentor proud."

Larry replied, "You didn't let me off the hook, Len. You were a real mentor and leader. You were willing to tell me what I needed to hear and make me do what I needed to do."

"Speaking of making you do what you need to do. . . ." said Tom Davin, standing up. "I have a story to add to that."

Tom was a Harvard MBA and a former Marine Corps officer—smart, good-looking, and a leader in all capitals.

"I was working at Goldman Sachs," said Tom, "the number one, most prestigious investment bank in the world, when one day I received a call from a recruiter. He told me that there was a guy from PepsiCo named Len Schutzman I had to meet. I was happy with my job and on the fast track to becoming a partner at Goldman Sachs, but because of Len's reputation on Wall Street and what I'd heard about him as a manager, I decided to take the interview.

"He told me, 'Tom, if you want to stay on Wall Street, there's not an awful lot I can do for you, but if you want to become more than just a financial manager and expand your career possibilities, PepsiCo is the right place.' I took on the challenge and became the assistant treasurer for mergers and acquisitions. That was the best decision I ever made in my career. Len allowed me to use my talents and skills in ways I had not thought possible.

"We met on a regular basis, and I valued the time he spent with me. When I told him that I wanted to run a business and be more operational, he got me a position as the director of Pizza Hut in Mobile, Alabama. I was responsible for seven Pizza Huts, but the first thing they made me do was clean the toilets. I couldn't believe it! I'd gone from assistant treasurer of PepsiCo to cleaning toilets! I called Len and told him, 'This is ridiculous. I wanted to be more operational, but not clean toilets.' Len, in his unique way, calmed me down and helped me understand that the manager wanted everyone to know what a clean toilet looks like, as it's an important indicator of a good restaurant. He was right.

"By learning what was involved and working my way up, I got a very good understanding of the business. With Len's mentorship, I became the Director of Operations for Taco Bell and eventually the President. Later, I was recruited by Panda, a private company, and I now own several companies. Besides the military and equipment and clothing companies, I recently started a new restaurant, Veggie Grill. Len's formula works for entrepreneurs, too. You have to develop the skills of a leader, whether you're in the corporate world, the non-profit sector, or are an entrepreneur. If I hadn't met Len and followed his eight-step guide to fast-tracking my career, I would likely still be a financial manager on Wall Street today. Thank you, Len. I would not have my current lifestyle if it weren't for you."

"My pleasure, Tom," I said. "You were one of the guys I always kept an eye on, just in case an opportunity presented itself to hire you back. You were great to work with."

The next person to speak was John Bronson, a seasoned human resources executive, having served as the top HR executive at several business units of PepsiCo and Williams Sonoma.

"Len has been a valuable asset for PepsiCo," he said, "and I never even worked for him. We were peers at Frito-Lay and PepsiCo. I learned a lot from Len about talent development by observing how he developed the financial organization in each of these businesses in a way that I never learned at HR, and I'm not a newbie in the industry. I've spent more than thirty years of my professional career in talent and leadership development. The results show that the Eight Step guide to fast-tracking your career works, regardless of your function. The proof is in the pudding. I have followed the career progression of many individuals coached by Len at PepsiCo, and I am overwhelmed by their accomplishments. We've just met a few of them here today, but there are many more. Every person Len mentored had some amazing raw talent, and I am convinced that Len made a big difference in their ultimate success."

"Thank you for your kind words, John," I said. "It certainly was a pleasure working with you."

At this point, I was getting a little shy from all the acknowledgments. A few more people shared their stories before dinner was served. Dave, the owner, had created the menu especially for me. It was beautiful and delicious. Everyone had a great time, and it was a nice opportunity to build relationships, as I had taught each one of my mentees the various parts of the Eight Step guide. Successful CEOs, CFOs, and other executives from big companies mingled and connected.

Around 1 a.m., the crowd began to thin out. There were a lot of hugs, more warm words of appreciation, and promises to stay in touch and get together from time to time. Larry Bouts came over to say goodbye. "This was one hell of an evening, Len! How great to see so many friends and colleagues who love and respect you."

"I felt embarrassed by all the accolades, Larry," I said. "Obviously, there was a great deal of raw talent, and it was a privilege to help develop that talent. Without question, mentoring each one of you was the highlight of my career. I'm very glad that you and Larry Meyer took the initiative when you saw the opportunity to enhance your careers by becoming part of the international bottling turnaround. Instead of waiting for a call from some HR guy, you decided to reach out to me directly. I respect that type of initiative. It put you both in key positions that allowed for rapid career progression in international businesses. It was a challenging project, but by working together, we made a big difference. It was great to have you on the team."

"It was a great project to be part of," Larry replied. "Looking back on your many years of experience, what would you say determines a financial professional's success?"

"Good question, Larry. In every organization with which I've been involved, whether as an employee, a consultant, or a member of the Board of Directors, there was always a strong correlation between business success and a strong, impactful financial function. That is why a financial professional who wants to be successful needs the following key qualities: Have integrity, be data-driven, and objectively present information. When you think outside the box, you can challenge conventional thinking, and identify risks or soft spots in the business analysis. Not to show off a 'gotcha attitude' or to prove that you know better than everyone else, but to improve decision-making throughout the organization.

"It's important to recognize that, regardless of your functional discipline, you have to expand your business knowledge and acumen by staying on top of competitive activities, by regularly listening to investor webcasts available on the Internet and by cultivating a wide network of outside contacts.

"And while not every company may place as much emphasis on the development of talent as PepsiCo, being able to attract, develop, and retain exceptional talent represents an important credential in being considered for senior leadership promotions.

"Developing future leaders needs to be made a priority. Even early in my career, I volunteered to accompany our recruiters on their campus visits, so I could possibly identify high-potential talent for my team or other functions. In my networking, I was always on the lookout for high potential talent that appeared to be a good fit for PepsiCo.

"Each year, I prepared development plans for myself and each of my direct reports and made sure that I had the buy-in of the employees and my superiors. Because of the importance of broadening one's horizons, I sought out appropriate developmental opportunities. I regularly asked for '360-degree feedback,' to understand not only what my superiors were thinking, but to also get the opinions of my employees. The more I was seen as a source of financial talent for the organization, the brighter my star seemed to shine within PepsiCo.

"There are a lot of young guys like you who are very smart and eager to learn, but just need a little guidance in their development. You can and should develop the ability to spot people who have the characteristics to excel. Be on the lookout for high-potential performers to develop. Stay close to professors and colleges to recruit young talent. Excel at attracting the best people, developing them, and building an effective team. Be known as someone who develops future leaders.

"Did you hear that Larry Bouts hired PepsiCo veteran Art Winkelblack as his CFO at Six Flags and that he later became CFO of Heinz? It's very exciting to see that my formula was taken on by my protégées and used to create a second generation of leaders. Likewise, Dave Rader used this formula to develop Bob Ryder, his controller, to become the CFO of Constellation Brands. They developed their own talent by applying the Eight Steps.

"The bottom line is that you must be proactive in managing your career and become known as someone who develops future leaders if you want to fast-track the corporate ladder."

Larry laughed. "It's true. After I took a proactive approach and contacted you for the international bottling project, my career skyrocketed, and many new doors of opportunity opened. I've learned a lot from you in the process, Len. So, what are you planning to do next? You're not the type of guy who sits at home all day watching television or playing cards."

"You got that right," I said. "I have great plans. My next project will be to capture my experiences and the lessons I've learned in a book. The book will provide a roadmap for aspiring young graduates entering the workplace, as well as help rejuvenate managers whose careers are stuck in neutral."

"That is a fantastic idea!" Larry said. "I know from my own experience that you have valuable information to share."

STEP #8. TAKEAWAY!

An effective leader is measured by his ability to recruit and develop high-talent players and direct them in superior execution. Being viewed as an effective coach with outstanding leadership skills is essential if you want to become a fast-tracker. One of the best ways to develop and display those skills is by identifying, mentoring, and grooming outstanding talent to become leaders within your company. By doing so, you create the ultimate win-win situation—you add value to the company, value to the careers of those you identify and develop, and you display the leadership skills that can only accelerate your life on the fast track!

Now that I've led you through the Eight Steps, I'd like to finish my story by looking at the importance of finding a balance between work and life. When you're on the fast track, it can come with a price. Is that price worth it? Can we find a balance between high achievement and the demands of our personal lives?

Read on. . . .

Chapter Ten

Work and Life Balance

After I had the stroke in 1992, my children became very close to me. My daughter left college to stay with me during my recovery. Now that I was no longer working, I had a lot of time to reflect back on my career, the great successes I had, and the trade-offs I had to make to achieve that success.

Both of my kids turned out great, but you need to be aware that there is a price to pay on the fast track. At first, it was hard to for me confront how my family was affected by my career. My children and I had an all-nighter where we talked about our family and their feelings about how my career had affected them. Because I had a good job, I could take my family to London every year, and my children told me how much they enjoyed those trips. But the other side of it was that I missed every school play, most of the soccer games, and a lot of other things. When we talked about this and got our feelings out into the open, it brought us even closer together.

My son has made different choices in his life. "There's no way I'm working in a corporate environment," he says. "I want to work, but I want to be home every day." And he's the best father—the father I wish I had been.

I came to realize that the fast track life isn't for everyone, and I feel it's my responsibility to let others know this.

I reflected more on this issue when Gary Bischoping and his wife Jeanine came by to have dinner and talk to me about the trouble they were having in balancing Gary's career with their family life. I first met Gary in 1996 at the Simon School of Business in Rochester, N.Y. while he was working on his MBA. He became my teacher's assistant in the Entrepreneurship class I was teaching there.

During our dinner together, we talked for a long time. They were a young couple, and I told them that they had to be careful about missing time with their kids. Several weeks after our meeting, Gary sent me the following letter.

Dear Len,

Little did I know how you would change the path of my life. My wife Jeanine and I are forever grateful for your simple act of kindness that we are now trying to pay forward.

You offered to take Jeanine and I out to dinner just before I was due to graduate from the Simon School and move to New York City to start my job at Stern Stewart and Co. as a consultant. We had a great time. As the dinner was wrapping up, you said, "Gary and Jeanine, look at the left side of my body. There is no job or amount of money that is worth losing the left side of your body. Even though I loved my job, I paid a high price. You have a choice to make. Your family, health, and happiness are worth more than any job or sum of money you will ever make. Please do not let the stress of work take over your life."

Jeanine and I talked about what you said that evening and developed a simple mantra that we've used for the last fifteen years: "I work to live, and I do not live to work." Your words of wisdom became the foundation of the four key principles to keep a good work/life balance, and I want to share them with you, as they may help other people you encounter as well.

At the time, Jeanine and I had been married for just over four years. We did not have any kids and didn't plan on starting a family until we had traveled the world for a few years. Jeanine was already apprehensive about me taking the job at Stern Stewart, as it was going to require me to travel over 70 percent of the time to the clients I would be consulting. But we had also stacked up a fair bit of student loan debt as Jeanine went back to school to earn her teaching degree while I was attending the Simon Business School. We agreed that once we had paid off our student loans, we would reconsider my job as a consultant and the associated lifestyle of travel and long hours.

We realized that it was important to talk about work/life tradeoffs and make a conscious decision about our career approach at that point in our lives. We certainly still had our moments when I was "working too much" while at Stern Stewart & Co., but it was a little easier to manage our way through, as we knew it was a temporary tradeoff. It kept us on the same page most of the time. Every year, we reflect on where we are in our life and where we plan to go.

Now, with our agreement in place, we moved to New York City, and I started my new job. One of the first major tests of your words of wisdom was about one year into my career at Stern Stewart & Co. The company had asked me to consider moving to Tokyo to start a new satellite office. We would commit to living in Tokyo for at least two years. It was a great opportunity to materially advance my career and accelerate my path to partner. Needless to say, I was very excited. At the time, I was traveling back and forth to Tokyo a lot and was staying for two to three weeks at a time, so I thought this opportunity would enable me to slow down my travel and spend more time with Jeanine and the new addition to the family who was due to be born in about two months.

But when I shared with Jeanine what an amazing opportunity this was, she wasn't aligned with my great idea. In fact, she ran upstairs and threw herself on the bed and said, "I am not having my first baby outside of the U.S. without my family around." Despite my persistence in arguing my points, it became very clear that this wasn't going to happen. I broke it to Stern Stewart that I wasn't going to take the opportunity in Tokyo. The company was disappointed, as was I. Jeanine had our first son, Jackson Smith Bischoping, in September 1998. After a couple of weeks of spending time with my son and seeing the joy he brought to the entire family, I realized that Jeanine had been absolutely right. Staying in our house in Long Island and continuing to work in New York City had been the right choice.

This situation taught us that we had to keep our priorities in order and keep them centered in our lives. We still have them in place today—family, faith, and fun. Keeping our priorities in front of us is the rudder that keeps us balanced and on track over time.

When my wife became pregnant with our second child, she sat down with me and said, "It's time to talk about our agreement. We agreed to reconsider our lifestyle once we paid off our student loans." I made it clear that we hadn't fully paid off our student loans yet and my career at Stern Stewart was progressing nicely, explaining that we were making a lot of money and I was really enjoying traveling around the world advising companies. Jeanine told me, in no uncertain terms, "You can either find a job where you can spend more time with your young family, or you can have your career without us."

I didn't see this coming, and it literally set me back in my chair. I realized she was serious and that this was an inflection point in our lives. Jeanine's clarity of thought and conviction jarred me back to our priorities—family, faith, and fun. We agreed that I would start looking for a new job that would allow me to be home for dinner and travel less so I could be with my wife and children.

Fifteen years later, I am still working at Dell in Texas. Jeanine and I have three wonderful kids and a tremendous support network, including our family and friends. It's that support network that is able to alert you when you are out of balance and can help you get back in balance—if you're willing to listen. We continue to live by our mantra: "I work to live, and I do not live to work." For our family, that means taking great family vacations that create lasting memories.

During these trips, I go out of my way to stay off email, with no texting or phone calls. I am certainly not perfect at this, but I have improved over time and now feel very confident asking my team to step up and cover things while I am out of the office. This proves to my employer that I have built a great team and I can count on them. Of course, when they take a vacation, I will cover for them.

Finding and sustaining work and life balance isn't easy. It took us time to figure out the right balance for us and how we could make it work. Jeanine and I have lived out what you impressed upon us during that special dinner in June, 1997, and it has made our family strong and happy. Thank you for the joy you have brought to our family.

I would not have wanted to miss seeing my boys grow up for anything in the world.

Best regards,
Gary E. Bischoping Jr.

Gary's letter touched me greatly. I was happy that I had made a positive impact on his life and the lives of his family.

TAKEAWAYS!

I have no regrets about my corporate career. Thanks to the Eight Steps, I reached heights I never imagined possible. But the reality is that there are personal costs that go along with the fast track. You have to be aware of that. Everyone will have a different attitude and experience with that reality, but the reality exists.

Based on what Gary told me in his letter, there are four key tools to find and sustain a good work-life balance.

Takeaway No. 1: Talk about work-life tradeoffs with your family and come to an agreement based on where you are at that point in your life and where you want to go. Revisit your agreement regularly.

Takeaway No. 2: Have your priorities in order and keep them centered in your life.

Takeaway No. 3: Have a great support network around you to make sure you stay focused on your priorities.

Takeaway No. 4: Be passionate about what you do and work hard at it, but take time to truly unplug and reap the rewards of your hard work.

The fast track is a great place to be, but, as with any achievement in life, there is a cost involved. Be clear about what that price is and whether you're willing to pay it.

CHAPTER ELEVEN

LIFE AFTER PEPSICO

After I suffered the stroke, Michael Jordan was one of the few senior PepsiCo executives who visited me regularly. Since we both loved Chinese food, he would often show up at my house with a feast from the best Chinese restaurant in town. Michael was a good friend, and he helped me realize that what Larry Bouts had told me was true: "You can't be in a club where they don't want you as a member."

PepsiCo had represented such a big portion of my life that I was shocked when they appointed a new treasurer, fearing that the stress of the job might be injurious to my health. But what was I going to do? They did provide a long-term disability package that assured my financial security.

It is said that when one door closes, another opens, and that turned out to be true. Bored sitting at home, I was delighted to receive a call from the Dean at the Simon Graduate School of Business, inviting me to serve as Executive-in-Residence, occasionally teaching a class and advising students. I did this for several months and enjoyed it immensely. I subsequently joined the faculty as executive Professor of Business and began regularly designing and teaching Strategy and Entrepreneurship classes to MBA students.

I brought the real world into the classroom by writing case studies on strategic issues at PepsiCo and then inviting the leaders of those business units to participate in the class discussion. What I enjoyed most was coaching and advising students. I have remained close to several students after they graduated, periodically taking calls from them on business and career issues. I am proud that many of them have gone on to successful careers in important businesses and Wall Street firms.

Out of the blue, I next received a call from my old Frito-Lay colleague Jim O'Neal, who was on the Board of the National Minority Supplier Development Council, a group of Fortune 500 companies dedicated to expanding minority supplier opportunities at large corporations. They had decided to create the Business Consortium Fund (BCF) to assist minority suppliers in growing their businesses, and they were looking for a Chairman. Jim thought I had the perfect background and wanted to recommend me for the position.

I was fortunate to be selected, and I began meeting with groups of minority suppliers and purchasing managers at our investor companies. It quickly became obvious to me that a major impediment to increasing business with minority suppliers was the lack of adequate productive capacity. Many of the suppliers were relatively small and had limited access to capital. The suppliers were hesitant to expand without firm indications of orders. To address this, we met with representatives of the Fortune 500 companies and asked them to nominate suppliers who would be eligible to receive more business if they expanded manufacturing. As a condition for the BCF to grant a loan to the supplier, we requested a multi-year purchase order, setting forth their projected repurchases from that vendor.

We then worked with each minority supplier to put together their business plan and financials for expanded production capacity. If everything was in order, we took the loan request to the BCF Investment Committee. In certain cases, we required the supplier to take additional business and management classes so they could provide the expertise necessary to run a larger operation. In a few cases, it was recognized that a merger of two smaller suppliers was the best way to provide both the scale and management expertise in order to supply a larger corporate account, and we worked to engineer these transactions. We also selected mentors from BCF's Board and managers to work with minority suppliers.

A few months later, I received another unexpected opportunity. With the growing popularity of online auction sites, a former business associate approached me about working with an entrepreneur who had a plan for an online travel auction website, Skyauction.com. He was looking for an advisor to assist in refining the business plan, raising capital, and, ultimately, taking the company public. I agreed to join the team in exchange for an equity stake. Raising capital for an early stage company with limited financial history was very different than accessing capital for PepsiCo. Nevertheless, I was able to gather a group of venture funds and angel investors to provide the necessary funding. Unfortunately, other companies such as Priceline and Travel Zoo developed faster and went public. Sky Auction still exists as a small private company.

After my wife and I agreed to a divorce, I decided to move to California to work with two teams of entrepreneurs, one interested in creating a frozen protein bar and the other in developing online software to place advertising. At the frozen protein bar company (Cold Fusion), one of the other advisors was Dr. Marcus Elliott, a leader in sports medicine and founder of the Peak Performance Institute (PPI), which primarily worked on rehabbing elite professional athletes.

Marcus thought that his rigorous conditioning program might be able to make a difference in my walking, so I would no longer need a heavy leg brace. This would only be feasible, in Marcus's view, if I stayed at least a month at his facility in Santa Barbara. I would spend a minimum of four hours per day at PPI doing a series of exercises and then another few hours on my own, walking and doing other strength training. Marcus had never used his protocol with a handicapped stroke victim, but he thought that my dedication and perseverance made it worth a try.

This was definitely the most intense and challenging rehab program I had ever done. Marcus was used to driving athletes to achieve results, and he was relentless. The exercises were extremely tough. Because one side of my body was paralyzed, it was very challenging to remain on my feet when using the balance ball or the elliptical machine. The pro athletes who were training there found this amusing and occasionally pleaded with Marcus to ease up on me. He didn't, and I just kept at it.

After the second week, Marcus said it was time to get rid of the leg brace.

While I was fearful that I might fall and break something, with his encouragement I was walking without a brace. After formal workouts each day, I would spend another few hours walking around the neighborhood. When I left a month later, I was a different person—I now had the confidence that I would overcome the handicaps and significantly improve the quality of my life.

And so, when I heard about a doctor in Southern California who was experimenting with using hyperbaric oxygen treatment to stimulate brain development and reverse the negative effects of stroke, I decided to give it a shot. The protocols would require me to lie prone in a small, pressurized capsule for ninety-minute treatments, five days a week, while following a strict diet and undergoing daily blood chelation to filter my blood. The chelation worked very well, and the blood flow through my carotid artery became normal. Blockage in that artery had been the cause of the stroke. However, the hyperbaric results were not positive. As a result of this testing, it was concluded that hyperbaric oxygen treatment, to be successful, must be deployed shortly after the event. In my case, almost a year had passed since the stroke.

With the birth of my first grandchild, I realized that living so far away was not conducive to being a good grandparent, so I moved back to Connecticut. Building on my positive experience at the Simon Business School, I began teaching classes in entrepreneurship at my alma mater, Queens College, where I created The Schutzman Center for Entrepreneurship, with the mission to inspire, equip, and empower the next generation of entrepreneurs. Working with creative students, faculty, and alumni gave me a great deal of personal satisfaction. PepsiCo provided part of the funding, under the PepsiCo Foundation Matching Gift Program, to launch The Schutzman Center.

And I'm not finished yet. I'm involved in several interesting, transformational entrepreneurial projects, lecturing MBA and undergraduate business programs, and writing two more books.

Yes, everyone, there is life after PepsiCo.

CHAPTER TWELVE

THE EIGHT STEP GUIDE TO TURBO CHARGE YOUR CAREER

In this chapter, I encourage you to immediately put the Eight Steps into action. After each step, I invite you to list the specific actions you can take to fast-track your career.

Step #1. Take Control and Seize the Initiative. PepsiCo gave me three short days to determine whether the company ought to spend hundreds of millions of dollars to purchase Taco Bell. Even though I had never handled an assignment of that magnitude, I realized it was a once-in-a-lifetime opportunity that could change my career. And the same can happen to you. It's not true that an accountant can only be the head of accounting and not the CFO. My career is proof of that.

List the steps you can take to take control and seize the initiative:

_____
_____
_____
_____
_____
_____
_____
_____
_____
_____
_____
_____
_____
_____
_____
_____
_____
_____
_____
_____
_____
_____
_____
_____
_____

Step #2. Broaden Your Horizons. Be ahead of the game. Review competitors' websites, read publications, keep abreast of developments in your field, and learn as much about your business and the industry as possible. At the same time, learn how to establish connections with key colleagues. When you broaden your perspective using my techniques, you'll be able to anticipate and benefit from upcoming trends, which will turbo-charge your career.

List the steps you can take to broaden your horizons:

_____

_____

_____

_____

_____

_____

_____

_____

_____

_____

_____

_____

_____

_____

_____

_____

_____

_____

_____

_____

_____

_____

_____

_____

_____

_____

Step #3. Step up to the Challenge. Be willing to take on tough, non-traditional jobs or challenging situations that may seem daunting at first. That's what happened to me when I was called upon to address a financial reporting crisis in PepsiCo's international bottling units. By taking on these kinds of challenges, you can significantly enhance your reputation and set yourself apart from the crowd.

List the steps you can take to step up to the challenge:

_____
_____
_____
_____
_____
_____
_____
_____
_____
_____
_____
_____
_____
_____
_____
_____
_____
_____
_____
_____
_____
_____
_____
_____

Step #4. Integrity above All Else. Integrity is the bedrock quality for any senior executive. It means objectively providing the facts and "telling it like it is" without sugarcoating, no matter what the consequences might be. When you have integrity above all else, people will have confidence in you. It's the foundation for any successful career.

List the steps you can take to have integrity above all else:

_____

_____

_____

_____

_____

_____

_____

_____

_____

_____

_____

_____

_____

_____

_____

_____

_____

_____

_____

_____

_____

_____

_____

_____

_____

_____

Step #5. Get Involved in Acquisitions. By contributing to special projects in high-visibility areas, such as acquisitions and international business development, you can shine in the eyes of senior management and propel your career to new heights. That's what happened to me when I was involved in the Taco Bell acquisition and during many other acquisitions throughout my career.

List the steps you can take to get involved in acquisitions or international business:

_____
_____
_____
_____
_____
_____
_____
_____
_____
_____
_____
_____
_____
_____
_____
_____
_____
_____
_____
_____

Step #6. Build Strong Relationships with Your Network. It was not just the connections I made that contributed to my career; it was developing and nourishing those relationships, year after year, and finding ways to add value to them that made the difference. The people in your network are your conduits to the outside world. They can provide you with the knowledge that gives you power, if you apply the strategies I share.

List the steps you can take to build strong relationships in your network:

_____

_____

_____

_____

_____

_____

_____

_____

_____

_____

_____

_____

_____

_____

_____

_____

_____

_____

_____

_____

_____

_____

_____

_____

_____

Step #7. Learn from the Masters—Find a Mentor. Finding the right mentor was a key factor in my career success, and it can be the same in your career development and entry into higher management. I was fortunate to have had amazing bosses at PepsiCo, each considered a titan in his field. They taught me every aspect of the business. In addition, as a junior executive, you need to understand the etiquette, politics, and unwritten rules of your company's culture if you want to progress up the ranks. A mentor can help you do that.

List the steps you can take to take to find a mentor:

_____

_____

_____

_____

_____

_____

_____

_____

_____

_____

_____

_____

_____

_____

_____

_____

_____

_____

_____

_____

_____

Step #8. Attract and Develop Future Leaders. Developing future leaders not only benefits the company but will help you accelerate your ascent up the corporate ladder. Early in my career, I volunteered to accompany our recruiters on their campus visits to identify talent, and in my networking, I was always on the lookout people who would be a good fit for PepsiCo. The ability to attract, develop, and retain exceptional talent is an important factor in being considered for senior leadership promotions.

List the steps you can take to attract and develop future leaders:

_____
_____
_____
_____
_____
_____
_____
_____
_____
_____
_____
_____
_____
_____
_____
_____
_____
_____
_____
_____
_____

Additional Notes

About the Author

Len Schutzman has a unique combination of corporate and entre-preneurial experience.

He was a senior executive at PepsiCo for more than eighteen years. He served as chairman of the board of directors at the Business Consortium Fund, which provided growth capital to minority-owned businesses.

Len is an Executive Professor of Business Administration at the William E. Simon Graduate School of business and is managing director of Leonard Schutzman associates, which provides consulting services to emerging growth companies.

He was an operating executive and limited partner in the private equity fund Evercore Capital Partners, where he advised portfolio companies on business development and strategy.

Mr. Schutzman is the founder and chairman of the board of advisors of the Schutzman Center for Entrepreneurship at Queens College.

He has a B.A. degree from Queens College, an MBA from the University of Rochester, and is a CPA.

Acknowledgments

I am grateful to all my former colleagues at PepsiCo, whose support and loyalty enabled me to climb the ladder. And, of course, to my incredible group of bosses and mentors who showed me the way.

And to my PepsiCo colleagues, Larry Bouts, Cave Rader, Tom Galligan, Larry Meyer, Jay Kushner, and Bob Mayerson, who I was privileged to coach during the early parts of their careers and who kindly shared their insights.

And to my colleagues, Bob Carleton, John Flaherty, and John Bronson, whose recollections provided color and detail to events described in the book.

L.S.
March, 2016

Appendix One

Leonard Schutzman's Career Track Record at PepsiCo, Inc.

June, 1976: Hired as Assistant Corporate Controller, PepsiCo, Inc.

August, 1978: Promoted to Vice President and Chief Financial Officer, Taco Bell.

August, 1979: Promoted to Vice President and Corporate Controller, PepsiCo, Inc.

February, 1982: Promoted to Vice President and Chief Financial Officer, Pepsi Cola Bottling International.

January, 1983: Promoted to Senior Vice President and Chief Financial Officer, Pepsi Cola International.

May, 1986: Promoted to Senior Vice President and Chief Financial Officer, Frito-Lay.

January, 1987: Promoted to Senior Vice President and Treasurer, PepsiCo, Inc.

September, 1994: Placed on long-term disability after suffering a stroke.

Appendix Two

Individuals Mentored by Len Schutzman Who Became Senior Executives in Large Corporations

(Many Have Since Gone on to New Positions)

Tom Galligan, CFO of Pepsi Bottling Company and CEO of Papa Ginos.

John T. Cahill, CEO of Kraft Foods.

Martyn R. Redgrave, CFO of Carlson Companies. He was also the Executive VP and Chief Administrative Officer of Limited Brands.

Larry D. Bouts, CEO of Six Flags Parks. He was also President of Toys "R" Us International.

Matt McKenna, CEO of Keep America Beautiful.

Dave Rader, Chairman of Sabra Dipping Company.

Robert Mayerson, Chief Operating and Financial Officer at Eastern Mountain Sports and Controller and Treasurer of Staples.

Robert Rayner, CEO of Specialty Products (a portfolio company of Evercore Capital Partners).

Tom Summer, CFO of Constellation Brands; CEO of Advanced Publications.

Miguel Calado, CFO of Dean Foods and President of Dean Foods International.

Oswaldo Banos, CFO of America Online Latin America.

Larry Meyer, CFO of Toys "R" Us International, Gymboree, Forever 21, and currently President of Uniqlo U.S.

Don Blair, CFO of Nike.

Shauna King, CFO of Yale University.

Claudia Morf, CFO of Rodale Publishing and Treasurer of CBS.

James Tom Shilen, CFO of CBS News and Former Vice President and Controller of Sara Lee Corporation.

Jay Kushner, Senior Vice President, Global Tax and Finance, at Viacom.

Tom Davin, President of the Panda Restaurant Group.

Timothy J. Kahn, CFO of Dreyer's Ice Cream.

Rick Carucci, CFO of Yum Brands.

Robert E. Briggs, CFO of Kaiser Permanente.

Robert Thompson, CFO of Interpublic Group.

Bob Nazarian, Executive Vice President and CFO Merrill Corp., Treasurer of Northwest Airlines, CFO of Air New Zealand.

Paul McMahon, Treasurer of Unilever North America.

David Sagal, Vice President and Controller of Taco Bell; Senior Vice President and CFO of Horn & Hardart Restaurant Group, Hotel Controller of Mandalay Bay Resort and Casino.

Robert James Ditkoff, Senior Vice President, Finance and Tax, Danaher Corporation.

Phil Defgliesse Jr., Vice President of Finance of Safeway Stores, Seattle Division.

THE CAREER READINESS EDUCATION PROGRAM

As you know from reading this book, I have a passion for helping people succeed to the best of their abilities. To continue to further this goal, I have developed a new program to help prepare young people to reach their fullest potential in careers in the business world.

Many young people today are having a lot of trouble finding careers, and once they enter the work world, they often don't have the skills to perform well on the job. That's because many colleges don't know how to properly prepare young people for careers. The Career Readiness Education Program is designed to help address these problems, based on my Eight Step program.

Businesses are continually telling us that they can't find young people who have the right skill sets for the business world, whether it's communication skills or the ability to think and plan in a clear way. The problem is that there's very little real-world training in most college curricula. Students don't get their "hands dirty," so to speak, by doing projects that are related to the reality of the business environment.

To remedy this situation, we've created virtual internships to better prepare college students for business careers. We're working with a range of companies and with students in many colleges, including a lot of international students studying in the United States. Currently, over 500 students are involved.

If you are interested in finding out more about this program, visit our website: **www.CareerReadinessInstitute.com**

35033360R00089

Made in the USA
Middletown, DE
16 September 2016